CREATIVES
LEAD

Kickstart Your Leadership Career,
Build a Team of Rock Stars, And
Become the Envy of Other Leaders
in Only 12 Weeks.

By Eric H. Brown

WeirdBooks Publishing • Atlanta, Georgia

Published by WeirdBooks Publishing©, a division of WeirdGuy Creative Solutions©
Atlanta, Georgia 30338
weirdguycreative.com

Published 2021
Printed in the United States of America

ISBN-13: 978-1-7367593-0-1 (paperback)
ISBN-13: 978-1-7367593-2-5 (e-book)

Creatives Lead: Kickstart Your Leadership Career, Build a Team of Rock Stars, and Become the Envy of Other Leaders in Only 12 Weeks.
For more information, visit: creativeslead.com

Copyediting: Brooke Turbyfill
Proofreading: Matt Hale
Cover design: Seth Rexilius, WonderWild© at wonderwild.co
Interior design: WeirdBooks Publishing
Photography: Mr. Jeno Uche

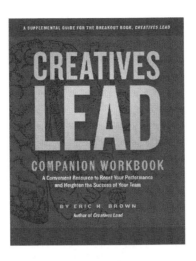

Increase Your Success as a Creative Leader

and Get The Companion Workbook—50% Off!

This must-have workbook includes the practical applications within *Creatives Lead* plus bonus materials. Use the tools in this convenient workbook to boost your performance and heighten the success of your team.

The workbook includes:

- Assessments and worksheets
- Interviewing templates
- Journaling pages
- Strategic off-site checklist
- To-Do / Not-To-Do Lists
- Exercises and more…

As my gift to you, I am offering this e-book for 50% off.

Go now to: creativeslead.com/workbookoffer

Contents

Part 4 - Now You Try It

Acknowledgements

Recommended Reading

Notes

About The Author

For Sharon,
My wife, my best friend, my muse.

Introduction

Jenn called.

"I am so frustrated!"

"What's going on?" I asked.

"Since you were last here, I now have twice the budget *and* twice the amount of people, but I can only get *half* the work done. I don't know what's going on. Got any ideas? It's so different now."

"Yes, it is different."

And so began our conversation.

This call and later conversations with new and seasoned leaders over the last 10 years prompted the idea for this book. How can creative people (creatives), who have been individual contributors for most of their career, successfully make the transition to leadership? Moving from a doer to leader (or as we used to say, "a worker bee to a suit") is a shift in mindset, skills, and values.

Most creatives want the chance for leadership. Some want it because of the salary increase. Some want it for the title and prestige. Others want it because of the new challenges it presents and the opportunity to help people, but most are not equipped or experienced to make the transition smoothly.

Why a Book About Creatives in Leadership

Creatives are different. They are primarily right-brainers. They vary between introverted and extroverted on how they're wired. They can be temperamental, complacent, whiny, my-way, and egotistical pouters. They can also be steadfast, giving, empathetic, problem solving, and self-sacrificing go-getters. Creatives come from a variety of backgrounds and careers: culinary, programming, architecture, writing, art, music, visual design, gaming, film, and more. They engage the world in a unique way. With a nod to Steve Jobs, cofounder of Apple® Computers, creatives "think differently" about work, relationships, life, spirituality, and the world at large. Managing can be a joy or can be drudgery. A lot of it is up to you. My hope is that this book will give you key insights and resources as you set sail into the often choppy but rewarding waters of creative leadership.

How This Book Is Organized

This book is broken into four parts that build on each other, each part composed of three weeks of reading. Each week has practical applications to put into practice as a new leader or manager.

The four parts are fashioned after Bruce Tuckman's stages of group development: forming, storming, norming, and performing.[1] Tuckman said that these stages were inevitable for all teams to go through to grow and become high performing. It is worth noting that any time a team is added to or a member is removed, these stages restart. How long it takes a team to cycle through these stages depends on the team makeup and the leader.

Part 1 is learning about the team, the team dynamics, adding and removing from the team, and preparing for a team off-site.

Part 2 is focusing on you as a leader, adjusting your mindset, learning habits, and modeling values to propel you successfully forward.

Part 3 is helping you and the team normalize, maintain focus, and gain momentum.

Part 4 is creating long-term culture, thinking ahead, and building future success for you and the team.

If you are new to leadership with little training or mentoring, you may want to read Part 2 before starting Part 1. If you have had some training and are now stepping into a full-time leadership role, I encourage you to read this book from front to back, as each week and each practical application build upon each other.

I have intentionally made the chapters bite-sized, so you can eat the meat and not worry about the bones. As you apply what you learn, be creative—put your spin on it—but above all, put it into practice.

Feel free to share with me your wins, recommendations, and frustrations. Leave a comment at www.creativeslead.com.

Enjoy!

Creatives Lead

Part 1

Let's Get Together

In this first part you are going to learn about the team, understand the team's dynamics, adding and removing from the team, and preparing for your first strategic team off-site.

Week One

Treat People the Way You Want to Be Treated

"Seek to understand before being understood" as Stephen R. Covey is often quoted. You will spend this week getting to know the team—their strengths, weaknesses, hopes, and dreams.

Week Two

Look People in the Eye

Building trust is tantamount to creating a high-performing team. This week you will learn to show respect, competence, and that you care about the team. You will also schedule a strategic off-site meeting three to four weeks in advance.

Week Three

Use Your Words

You will prepare for your upcoming strategic team off-site meeting. You will be setting clear expectations, reviewing the role of communication, and establishing accountability for the months ahead.

Creatives Lead

Treat People the Way You Want to Be Treated

"Seek to understand before being understood" as Stephen R. Covey is often quoted. You will spend this week getting to know the team—their strengths, weaknesses, hopes, and dreams.

- Put Yourself in Their Shoes
- Temperament Types for Creatives
- When Hiring
- When Dismissing
- Week 1 Practical Applications

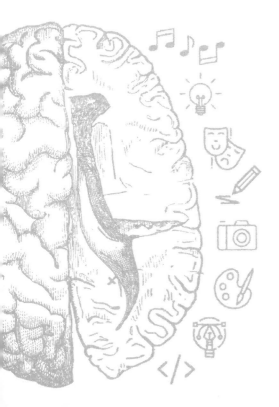

Creatives Lead

Chapter 1
Put Yourself in Their Shoes

Carol had been doing her job for some time when she learned she had a new manager. As the manager got to know Carol, the manager was impressed by her hard work ethic and all she had done for the company. Her new manager wanted to be encouraging and told Carol she was going to try and get her a title change and salary bump—at least a bonus for all her hard work. Unfortunately, the well-meaning manager spoke too soon. After trying to get the money approved, the request fell through. Carol had been excited about the possibility. She had been working hard to demonstrate her worth, waiting with expectancy for an increase or title change with bonus. When Carol learned the money had not been approved, she was totally demoralized. As a result, she started looking for work in another area.

This story doesn't mean that if you make a mistake your employees are going to hop online and start sending out resumes. It *does* mean that, as a leader, you need to be careful what you say and do. What may seem like a "whisper" from you is often heard as a "shout" from your creative staff. Put yourself in the place of your employees. You were recently there. How would you feel? What would you think or do if this happened to you? Would you feel let down or even betrayed?

Do you know your people well enough to know what is happening in their lives? If performance starts to slip with Joe, is it because Joe is slacking or because Joe is not challenged at work? It could be because Joe's wife had a baby, and they are not getting much sleep. It could be one of his children had an accident that has put a major financial strain on the family. These situations will impact Joe's performance.

You may be thinking, "Well, Joe needs to separate work from home," or "Joe should not bring his personal issues to work." After all, that's what management has taught in the past—to which I say, REALLY?! Show me someone who can separate themselves from their feelings, and I'll show you a robot. If you want a robot to do the work, get rid of the people. I hear AI (Artificial Intelligence) is improving as a technology.

You have to learn to put yourself in the shoes of your employees. You need to learn to empathize. Get to know *them*, not just *about* them.

"Say What You Mean - Mean What You Say"

As a new leader, you may be tempted to acquire what you wished for before you were in management. Giving that raise to Keisha, upgrading the software for the team, replacing the "ancient" monitors the designers are using, and the list goes on. Unfortunately, what you will find is an operational approval process that will ask you to make a business case for each of these expenses.

Welcome to "administrivia" and the world of "operational red tape."

Now, before you get frustrated, these processes are needed so your company stays profitable, you get paid, and your team members have jobs. This is where the rubber meets the road, and you as a leader need to be very careful about what you say or promise to your team.

Early in my career as a leader, I made this same well-meaning mistake. I wanted what was best for my team. I wanted to reward their hard work. I wanted to make sure they had the tools needed to do their jobs. I did not check to see if these kinds of things were budgeted. Even though I did not promise these things, the fact that I even mentioned them created a false hope in my team that was dashed when I later learned I could not get items approved. This impacted morale and the level of trust the team had in me. I had to learn to find a balance between encouraging the team and rewarding them. The bottom line: do not make commitments at the beginning that you may not be able to keep. While good intentioned, it sets up false hope that will dishearten team members.

Getting To Know You

Take the time to get to know your team. Learn how they function individually and as a group. This takes effort and being intentional about getting below the surface layer.

You may look at skill assessments or temperament tests as fun ways to learn more about your team. You may schedule informal lunches or happy hours to get to know your people away from the workplace. The sooner you get to know the team, the sooner you will be able to measure their level of engagement, their capacity, and how to align certain members to certain projects. You'll also gain a higher level of empathy and build trust that can quickly set you off in the right direction as a leader.

In the next chapter, we will explore temperament assessments as one way to get to know your individual team members and your team mix as a whole. This is also a fun way to engage the team in the upcoming off-site meeting that you'll soon be planning.

Creatives Lead

Chapter 2

Temperament Types for Creatives

"You are such a Gamer."

"Yes, and you are a big-time Architect."

"I like to have things in order and to be on time. For you, time is not that big a deal. That's why I am always the timekeeper."

"Not always."

"True. Once last year you were on time." Laughter.

"Well," I said to our visiting friends, "as you can see, she has tightened me up, and I have loosened her up. Instead of pulling away from each other, we have moved toward each other. We have learned to lean into each other's strengths."

When it comes to temperament frameworks, most have heard of Ned Herrmann's Whole Brain, Galen's Four Temperaments, the DiSC® assessment, and the Keirsey Temperament Sorter. One of the lesser known frameworks, but just as insightful, is the *Creatives Lead Temperament Types©*. The temperaments are based on creative industries and characteristics. Not only are these temperament types entertaining, but they also are very simple for people young and old to grasp.

While these temperament types are broad categories, I find them easy to associate and communicate. This is extremely beneficial when dealing with employees and/or people in general. Knowing employee temperaments can make the work environment, meetings, projects, and relationships run more smoothly.

Living in the Creative Kingdom

Listed below are the characteristics of each creative temperament and how they line up with Galen's and the DiSC for comparison:

Entrepreneur Temperament - Choleric/Dominance

Associated Names: The Creative Director, Influencer

Strengths: Visionary, practical, productive, strong-willed, independent, decisive, leader

Weaknesses: Cold, domineering, unemotional, self-sufficient, unforgiving, sarcastic, cruel

Entertainer Temperament - Sanguine/Influence

Associated Names: The Chef, Networker

Strengths: Outgoing, responsive, warm, friendly, talkative, enthusiastic, compassionate

Weaknesses: Undisciplined, unproductive, exaggerating, egocentric, unstable

Gamer Temperament - Phlegmatic/Steadiness

Associated Names: The Drummer, Collaborator

Strengths: Calm, easygoing, dependable, quiet, objective, diplomatic, humorous

Weaknesses: Selfish, stingy, procrastinating, unmotivated, indecisive, fearful, worrying

Architect Temperament - Melancholy/Compliance

Associated Names: The Programmer, Contributor

Strengths: Analytical, self-disciplined, industrious, organized, aesthetic, sacrificing

Weaknesses: Moody, self-centered, touchy, negative, unsociable, critical, revengeful

The Temperament Grid

Looking at the grid below, it is interesting to learn how the top row tends to be extroverted in how these types of people express their thoughts and emotions, while the bottom row tends to be introverted. Similarly, the left column tends to be people-oriented, while the right column tends to be task-oriented.

ENTERTAINER	ENTREPRENEUR
GAMER	ARCHITECT

In Kathleen Edelman's workbook, *I Said This, You Heard That,* she discusses the need to understand not only your "language" but the "language" of others to communicate more effectively.

"There are four temperaments, each predisposed to speak (and hear) certain words. It may be helpful to think of your temperament as your first (or native) language. It's what comes naturally to you," Kathleen says.[2]

An *Entrepreneur* Temperament will have differing expectations and communication styles than a *Gamer* Temperament. Understanding each other's unique needs and expectations will help make communication and teamwork better. We will cover that next, but first you will want to take your own assessment to learn your unique temperament.

Take the Assessment

This online assessment should take no more than five to ten minutes to complete. You can find it here by visiting: http://bit.ly/3bicte9

When you look at your results, you'll find that you have a primary type and a secondary type. Some naturally go together and make for a wonderful set of strengths.

Take a moment to reflect after taking the assessment. Which temperament type is your primary and which one is your secondary? Be confident in the strengths stated earlier, and be sensitive to the weaknesses.

Are there things you need to change? Ask a trusted friend, spouse, or significant other to review these with you. Ask them to tell you the truth of what they see and perceive as your strengths and weaknesses.

When you're ready, move on to the next section.

Understanding the Temperaments

In the last section we examined the strengths and weaknesses of each of the four temperaments—Entrepreneur, Entertainer, Gamer, and Architect. You were also given a chance to take a self-assessment to learn your primary and secondary temperaments. Which of the strengths did you see the most of in you? Which ones did you see the least of in you? From experience, I have seen this exercise as beneficial to creating successful teamwork, communication, and harmony in the workplace *and* home. Now, let's take a few minutes to understand some of the unique needs and desires of each temperament.

Entrepreneur "I need it now!", "Get to the point."

Their Environment: lots of projects, awards on the wall, large calendar, office furniture arranged neatly to demonstrate control

They Gain Security by: control

Their Pace: fast and decisive

They Need: a climate that responds

They're Irritated by: wasted time, unpreparedness, touchy-feely conversations, blocking results

Entertainer "Did you hear…?", "Relax!"

Their Environment: organized-cluttered, slogans on the wall, personal pictures, friendly and casual

They Gain Security by: flexibility

Their Pace: fast and spontaneous

They Need: a climate that is fun and collaborates

They're Irritated by: too many facts, boring and repetitive tasks, same old approach, routine, being alone, ignoring their opinions

Gamer "Keep it steady.", "Let's work together!"

Their Environment: group pictures, catchphrases on the wall, personal items and toys, relaxed and inviting decorations

They Gain Security by: close relationships

Their Pace: slow and steady

They Need: a climate that processes

They're Irritated by: pushy and aggressive behavior, insincerity, being put on the spot, disrupting the status quo

Architect "Do it the right way!", "Show me the proof!"

Their Environment: structured and organized, charts and infographics, functional decor, practical seating arrangement

They Gain Security by: preparation

Their Pace: slow and systematic

They Need: a climate that describes

They're Irritated by: people who do not know what they are talking about, lack of attention to detail, surprises, unpredictability

How did the needs and desires for your temperament resonate with you? Your unique wiring comes naturally to you, but the other temperaments may not.

Understanding this framework is quite simple. Putting it into practice is a journey. It takes time and patience. As you begin to learn the temperaments of the team, you'll find a greater need to become "multi-lingual." You will also understand why intermingled teams perform better.

Interlude

Charles had spent five years building his small company. Over the last couple of years he had doubled the size of the organization to twenty-four employees. While more clients and projects were being acquired, deadlines were being missed. This caused frustration for employees and customers alike.

Charles was familiar with temperament assessments and had all the new hires take one. This was done in an effort to understand the style of each new company member. Now, as the company had grown, Charles sensed there were larger team dynamics at play that affected performance. He knew something had to change. While he had been keeping track of individual team temperaments, he never stopped to consider the mix of project teams nor the company overall.

The company retreat was around the corner. Charles invited Karen, a professional facilitator, to come in. He asked her to analyze and discuss the dynamics of the differing temperaments in regard to the team. Karen was given access to all the company assessments and the team assignments. On the day of the retreat, she shared her findings with the group.

"I do not know if you are aware, but two thirds of your company is made up of Architect and Gamer temperaments. This means you have a lot of processes you follow, and you pay attention to details. It also means you are easygoing and get along well," Karen said.

She showed a slide on the screen with a list of names in each quadrant. Startled murmurs ran around the room. There were only a couple names in the Entrepreneur and Entertainer categories. Of the twenty-four employees, the breakdown looked like this:

Entrepreneur = 3

Entertainer = 3

Gamer = 7

Architect = 11

Next, Karen showed a slide with the project teams broken down by temperament.

"Oh my!" gasped Charles.

"As you can see, the projects that are moving along and staying on track have a good mix of temperaments. The projects that have an imbalance are the ones that are struggling."

Levin, a self-professed Architect and account manager, stated, "I see some trends here. The projects I have been involved in have bogged down because of research and analysis. As new information has come in, we have spent time in evaluation. I am guessing too much time."

"Yes," Karen nodded. "And if you look at the projects that have moved forward, it has taken an Entrepreneur to keep it on track."

Everyone laughed nervously.

Over the remaining hour and a half, Karen guided the attendees through a discussion of the projects and blend of team temperaments. While it was challenging, the group was able to have a candid conversation about their various strengths and weaknesses. They also looked at the unique needs for each project to determine the best mix. Charles learned that putting together differing temperaments was not only a growth opportunity for the individuals, but also better for getting work out the door on time.

Communicating Amongst the Temperaments

Let's look at the communication strategies we can use when working with the "creative" temperaments. Becoming proficient in the various languages is essential with a mixed team. Listed below are ideas to help you better understand your teammates:

Working with the Entrepreneur (Choleric)

General Strategies:

Support their goals and aspirations - Let them know you have their best interests in mind, and you are there to uplift them and their efforts.

Argue facts and not feelings, if you disagree with them - They want to know your recommendations are backed with data and research.

Be exact - They like precision and for you to get to the point quickly.

Be time disciplined and organized - They want to know you respect their time and effort, so do not be late to meetings and come prepared.

Focus on the results, and do not waste their time - This pretty much speaks for itself.

Let them make the decision - They want to feel in control. While providing them with information and options are good, allowing them to decide the next step will make them feel valued.

Working with the Entertainer (Sanguine)

General Strategies:

Be interested in them - Show a genuine interest in them as a person and employee. Set aside a few minutes in meetings to ask them how they are and then listen intently.

Support their dreams, thoughts, and feelings - Ask them about their career goals and dreams and how you can help them. In meetings, they like to know they have been heard and that their thoughts and opinions matter.

Be sociable - Have team-building events and outings. Better yet, put them in charge of those events.

Do not rush the discussion; give them a chance to verbalize - They are verbal processors. Do not be shocked by what they say because they are processing their thinking out loud. Allow them the time and space to do this.

Don't drown them with details; put it all in writing - Unlike Architects, they deal more in generalities. They typically do not take notes (a growth opportunity), so be sure to delineate expectations and deadlines in writing.

Do not be shy or quiet - They are more extroverted and people-oriented, so you do not have to worry about being quiet or verbalizing your thoughts with them.

Follow up on the specifics of any arrangement - Don't speak in generalities if something needs to be done. If you need something done by two o'clock on Wednesday, let them know and make sure you agree on the details. As noted above, a follow-up in writing is helpful.

Working with the Gamer (Phlegmatic)

General Strategies:

Be non-threatening and sincere - Because they are easygoing, there is no need to be severe with them. Be upfront about your desires and expectations when communicating with them.

Show personal interest and be supportive; don't push - They understand what is expected of them, so there is rarely need to push. Like the Entertainer, they want to feel appreciated and understood.

Move along in a calm manner - This does not mean sacrificing high pace, but as you communicate, be thorough, intentional, and relaxed. They can be empathetic, and if you show anxiety, they will pick up on it and become anxious as well.

Demonstrate that you are listening - We will discuss listening in detail in Week 3, but Gamers want to know you are engaged in the conversation. They are looking at your eyes, body language, and the responses you give as indicators of your attention.

Be easygoing - This is not easy for some. It is more of a learned attitude. It is the ability to stay calm in the midst of uncertainty or change.

Assure them that you stand behind their decisions - This does not mean they can do whatever they want. Being more introverted, they will be thoughtful and not make rash decisions. They will appreciate that you have their back.

Working with the Architect (Melancholic)

General Strategies:

Be thorough and well prepared - Like the Entrepreneur, they want to know you respect their time so come prepared for meetings and give details priority.

Be supportive of their thoughtful approach - They are very inquisitive and thorough. They approach all their work with a disciplined process. Learn to understand this and support them.

Demonstrate through your actions, not words - Because they are so task oriented, they prefer action over talk. If you do say you are going to do something, be sure to follow up or risk being diminished in their eyes.

Be exact and organized - If you are not exact in your information and data, you may get called out. They want you to be precise and prepared. They will have little patience if you are not prepared.

Give them time to verify - Because they value correct information, they may need additional time to research and verify what has been presented. It is not a lack of trust as much as it is their desire to know and learn.

Don't rush their decision making - As stated, they love (I mean *love*) research and analysis. If this needs to be rushed, be sure to give them an allotted timeframe to make decisions.

Avoid gimmicks - They can be very pessimistic when it comes to processes they perceive as trite or gimmicky. They value tried-and-true processes and methods. If you are implementing something new, give them time to adapt.

Provide evidence - This one speaks for itself. Like themselves, they want to know you too have done the research that is accurate and true.

I hope these tactics have been helpful and have added "tools" to your leadership and personal communication tool belt. As always, the application of knowledge is often the hardest part. Take what you've learned and proceed one step at a time. Even if you pick just one strategy to work on over the next couple weeks, you'll be pleasantly surprised at the results.

A final word before we move on. Like Charles learned to mix the temperaments in his company, look for ways to leverage the strengths and weaknesses of each type. If you are putting a task force together to come up with a new concept, don't only look at the various skills they bring to the table. Look at the mix of temperaments on the task force as well. Also, it can be valuable in a mentoring relationship to put opposite temperaments together. They can learn from each other and provide enriching feedback. Next, we will discuss the hiring process. Remember what you have learned here as you progress to the next chapter.

Chapter 3

When Hiring

How to Properly Assign New Employees

Put 400 bricks in a room. Put your new hires in the room and close the door. Leave them alone and come back after six hours. Then analyze the situation:

- If they are counting the bricks, put them in the Accounting Department.
- If they are recounting them, put them in Auditing.
- If they have messed up the whole place with bricks, put them in Engineering.
- If they are arranging the bricks in some strange order, put them in Planning.
- If they are throwing the bricks at each other, put them in Operations.
- If they are sleeping, put them in Security.
- If they have broken the bricks into pieces, put them in I.T.
- If they are sitting idle, put them in Human Resources.

- If they say they have tried different combinations and they are looking for more, yet not a brick has been moved, put them in Sales.
- If they have already left for the day, put them in Management.
- If they are staring out the window, put them in Strategic Planning.
- If they are talking to each other, and not a single brick has been moved, congratulate them and put them in Top Management.

Okay, enough fun and games. I hope I did not ruffle any feathers with that humorous analogy. This may have been running around the internet for a while, but I saw it and had to chuckle.

Why is hiring one of the first items we're reviewing? As a new leader, you may be faced with having to add or replace members on the team. When getting to know the team, you will quickly learn who are the keepers and who are the coasters. You will also learn who is looking for opportunities elsewhere and who needs extra learning and training to grow.

As a creative, you may be more introverted, and the thought of hiring makes you nervous. It may be something you have never done before or have had limited experience. For every new leader, hiring can feel daunting and laborious. Going through 50-100 resumes and portfolios could seem to take forever. Then comes the dreaded phone or face-to-face interviews. Both parties are putting their best foot forward. How do you keep from blowing it and hiring the wrong person? How do you hire quality, high-performing people?

The truth is: hiring is serious business. It can take a long time and be frustrating. Let me repeat that—it can take a long time and be frustrating. Why? Several reasons: 1) There's a talent war to get and retain the best people, 2) Resumes (and resume sites) can be gamed and misleading, and 3) The workers of today have seen how their parents' generation was treated, and they are not beholden to anyone but themselves—devotion to an employer is a thing of the past. So what is a new leader to do in these circumstances?

Addressing the Talent War

Creating Culture

Good talent can be hard to come by and harder to attract. Think about the culture you have within your organization, your department, and on your team. They are not all equal. What kind of culture are you creating? You can have a team culture that is different from your organizational culture. You really can! Great culture attracts great talent.

Culture Partitions

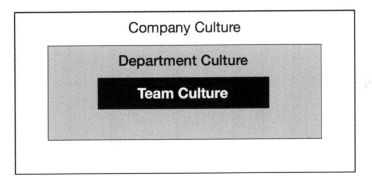

I remember when I was a new leader. I thought back on my previous managers and leaders (both good and bad) and determined how I wanted to create a different environment. I created an environment of collaboration, experimentation, fun, empowerment, and equality. It did not take long, and word got around the company that I was doing something different and it was getting results. People from around the organization were reaching out to see if they could work for me. I was creating a culture where the best wanted to work and told others about it.

Constant Networking

As you can see from the story above, the employees enjoyed the environment they were working in and became advocates. Not only did they talk about their work with other employees, but they talked to their friends and personal networks. They knew people who would be good additions to the team. They were talent scouting for the team without having to be asked!

Never underestimate the power of your network nor the networks of your team members. Strong performers attract strong performers. No matter what city you live in, nor the industry you work in, word gets around. People know each other, and they talk. What kind of conversation do you want them to have about you? Your team? Your company? Keep networking and keep your networks strong.

Adapt to new social networking sites that cater to your candidates. LinkedIn® is an obvious destination. Instagram®, Dribbble®, TikTok®, Artstation®, and even Twitter® are sites that younger creatives are using. See what's out there, set up an account, and build new networks.

One last point here regarding networking. Be intentional about looking for a diverse variety and candidate pool. Bring differing thoughts, experiences, ideas, and strengths into your team and organization. You cannot do all the work. Look for people who are strong where you are weak and not people that look and think like you (see chapter eleven).

Addressing Resumes

Gone are the days of paper resumes. Do you remember having to keep a resume to a minimum of two pages? Updating your resume was routine business. Now we have a variety of digital tools at our disposal to create and update our resumes. We also have access to thousands of other resumes, and we can copy and revise our own based on someone else's. We have learned the art of gaming our resumes to make us look like amazing A-player, rock star, super-ninja unicorns!

So what value is a resume to you for hiring? Well, it is often required by Human Resources. It is an advertisement for potential candidates and is the first line of screening for new hires. But, *understand* exactly what you are looking at. As Martin Yates says in his book *Hiring the Best:*

> Reading resumes is no one's idea of a good time. After half a dozen, even the strongest wills among us begin to approach a state of catatonia.[3]

If you don't want to get fooled, your first job is to find the cracks the different resume types are designed to hide. As the accepted objective of a resume is to generate enough interest to get an interview, you would be prudent to assume that the writer will put anything down that will help get a foot in the door.[4]

Some of those resume types are functional, chronological, project/STAR-based, and story-based using video and interactive elements.[5] Of this latter type, don't get sucked into the glitz and glamour of technology-based resumes. Find the cracks, as Yates says, and then decide which people you want to take to the next level of hiring—the phone screen or, if your HR department has done this for you, the face-to-face interview.

Online Portfolios and Video Highlights

Now, we will take a moment to discuss technology-based resumes and portfolios. Having photos and screenshots, audio samples of music or voice-over, video highlight reels, or apps that have been coded are minimum requirements. Below are some tips for reviewing digital portfolios and what to look for:

- How well is the portfolio designed? Is the design an extension of the candidate?
- How user-friendly is the portfolio? If the candidate is applying for a user experience (UX) role and the portfolio is difficult to navigate, what does that say about his or her skills and attention to detail?
- Does the portfolio weave a narrative about the candidate and his skills?
- Are audio and video files clean and well-edited?
- Are there examples of the candidate's writing to download?
- Is the candidate specific about the work she did on a project? The code she wrote?

- Are the photos and images optimized for the web?
- Does the candidate clearly articulate her process, approach, or methods?
- Is it clear how he or she solved creative problems?
- Is the portfolio clearly-written and typo-free?
- For junior creatives, does their potential come through?
- For senior creatives, do they demonstrate a mature skill set and variety of solutions?
- Does the portfolio reference business outcomes and successes?

Addressing Today's Worker

A couple generations back, it was not uncommon for a person to work for and retire from the same company. Unfortunately, capitalism put more of an emphasis on money than on people. As a result, cheaply-made products, layoffs, downsizing, and corporate hiking ensued. History tells the story well. More recently, there seems to be an emerging trend in business that recognizes the worth of stable, contributing, long-term employees, but the damage has been done. Today's workers no longer believe in the companies they work for. The bonds of trust were broken with their parents and grandparents. Added to the mix is a service-oriented digital economy where workers from around the world can be employed and work remotely.

Recruiting agencies run rampant across services like LinkedIn, offering better pay and promotions. I average several messages a week from recruiters asking me if I am satisfied with my current work environment and pay scale. This is the world your new employees live in. No wonder their resumes only show a couple years at each company. They are looking out for themselves and can move on a whim if they don't feel content or challenged.

You cannot let this bother you. It is the new norm. However, you can set expectations with new employees, and you should. They are making decisions about you as much as you are making decisions about them. Be up front. Don't hide the blemishes. A worthwhile and mature employee should know the grass is not always greener at another company. Every company has its issues.

Hiring and Interview Tips

Finally, here are a collection of tips I have collated over the years. I hope you find them helpful.

Hire Slow/Fire Fast

This is more of a principle than a tip. Take your time hiring. There is nothing worse than rushing to get a warm body to fill a seat only to find out later that you made a mistake. I understand there may be pressure to fill a position quickly. However, it is better to fill it with the best candidate than realize later that your new hire needs to be put on a performance plan.

If you do make a mistake, work with your HR team to see the best way to handle the situation. Consider a 30-day contract period to truly determine if the person has the skills and temperament to get the job done and is a good fit with the team. If the contractor is working out well, you can transition the contract role to full time. When hiring a full-time employee, make sure you meet with that person within thirty days of her start date. You can use this meeting to assess her progress, evaluate job competency, and see which resources, training, or tools she may need. If skill gaps or unproductive behavior exists, take quick and concrete action, including termination if necessary (more on termination in the next chapter).

Prepare a Questionnaire

You may have access to a questionnaire from your Human Resources department, or you can create your own. The key is to have one prepared in advance based on the job requirements, competencies, and cultural fit. This will be extremely useful in the interview, so you can focus on the answers versus stumbling over what question to ask next. You can always add additional questions during the interview if you desire to probe further on a particular item. In some cases, you may be required to use a specific questionnaire from Human Resources. If that is your situation, make sure you can squeeze in creative-specific questions as well.

Set the Stage and Tone

Let the candidate know what the role is they are applying for and your expectations. How you present yourself will determine how the candidate reacts. You can be all business, or you can be friendly and accommodating, but the best rule is to be yourself. You are creating the culture for the team—reflect that culture.

Past Behavior Can Be a Predictor of Future Behavior

Use open-ended questions to probe a candidate's past behaviors, accomplishments, and how they handled difficult situations. While it is true that people can change, under duress we tend to fall back on past, ingrained behaviors. Know the behaviors you seek in an employee and see if they exhibit those qualities. Create questions that elicit real-life examples. Instead of asking how *would* you, ask how *did* you.

Ask Open-ended Questions

As stated above, you want to use open-ended questions to get the candidate talking. People often love to talk about themselves, and the more you can get them to talk, the more you will learn. Open-ended questions generally start with *who*, *what*, *where*, *when*, *why*, and *how*. "Describe a time..." or "Tell me..." are also good ways to start open-ended questions. Closed (yes and no) questions should be reserved for simple job qualification questions: "Are you able to lift twenty-five pounds?" Etc.

Examples of powerful open-ended questions:

- How has your education and experience prepared you for this job?
- How necessary is it for you to be creative?
- Why do you want to work here?
- In your current (or most recent job), what was your greatest accomplishment?
- What are the major qualities this job demands?

- Describe a situation at your current (or past) job where you had to influence people on an approach or task?
- What lessons did you learn from a project that did not end well?
- Who caused you the most problems completing a project?
- How did you get your last job?
- Why did you leave your last job?
- If we were to make you an offer, what considerations would you have in terms of accepting the position? Probe further on other jobs they are in the running for. Avoid the money question as HR should have screened on these details, or maybe they have other personal conflicts in terms of timing.
- What questions do you have? Always allow ample time for questions. The contents of the candidates' questions can be as telling as their earlier answers. Also, remember they are "interviewing" you as much as you are interviewing them.

Learn How the Candidates Think and Approach Work

As you conduct the interview, it is often the case that a creative's portfolio reflects the final product of stakeholders. While all the work may not be the result of the candidate, you can and should find out how they approach work and their thinking process. This will tell you more than a series of pages, pictures, or websites.

As the candidate talks, does he provide the problem he was trying to solve? Does he talk about creating a plan? What was that plan? What actions did he or she take as a result of that plan? What was the final outcome of the project? Answers to these questions can provide a wealth of knowledge and separate the qualified candidates from the not-so-qualified.

Listen for "I" and "We" Statements

While you want a team player, you also need to know what the candidate did and how they uniquely contributed to a project. Listen for how often the candidate uses the words "I" or "We" and if he uses "I" too much. Listen further to see if he feels he is a "star" performer. Is that person going to be a good fit for your team? If the candidate uses "we" excessively, you may want to ask him specifically what he did on a project.

Probe Deeper/Layer Questions

This takes practice. It is as much of a skill as it is an art to probe behind the initial answer. For instance, you may ask: "Tell me about an unpopular decision you had to make."

You could certainly move on to another question from there, but look at how much more you could learn if you probed further with:

- Who did it affect?
- Why did the situation arise?
- How long did it take to make the decision?
- How do you feel you handled it?
- What did you learn from the event?
- What would you do differently next time?

Ask for Examples and Details

As stated above, don't let the initial answer be the only answer. Ask more questions. Ask candidates to be specific about what their role was on various projects or within their team. For example, if they are taking credit or being vague about who redesigned a website, it should come out in the conversation.

If required to ask specific questions in a determined order, work with HR ahead of time. You may need to get approval on any creative-centric questions to ask in order to make a discerning decision.

Ask 20/Listen 80

Learn to ask questions twenty percent of the time while listening eighty percent of the time during an interview. For this reason, it is critical that when creating your initial interview questions, keep them few yet powerful. You want to listen to the answers from the candidate as much as possible.

Keep the Interview on Track

Creatives can often run over time. You may have a candidate who cannot stop talking (that's his personality, or he's nervous) or one who is a fast talker, making it hard to get a word in edgewise. Don't let that distract you. Stay on task. Stay on time.

Don't Let a Candidate Off the Hook

I have seen and experienced getting flustered because the candidate did not have a prepared answer. Sometimes it seems easier to move on to another question. Don't do it. If it is a "throw away" question, it should not be part of your questionnaire. Give the candidate a moment, but don't let her off the hook. This tells you as much about the candidate as his or her answer does.

Take Good Notes

First, take good notes to refer back to because, after numerous interviews, you are likely to forget how people answered. Second, it's good for the candidate to see that you are taking notes and that you are taking what he or she has to say seriously. The candidate knows you mean business, and he should as well. However, be careful that your note taking does not distract you from fully listening to the candidate's responses. Focusing too much on your notes and not providing good eye contact with the candidate can make them more nervous than they are already.

Armed with these tips and resources, I know your interviewing will go much easier than my first ones did. Be sure to tailor your questionnaire to the job, the kinds of skills, and individual qualities you are looking for in a team member. Again, I cannot stress enough to work with your Human Resources department as much as you can. Finally, be willing to set aside time to practice using your questionnaire, so you can maximize the time with your candidates.

Legal Tips

I hate to bring the lawyers into this, but to ensure you have a legally defensible hiring practice, here are a few additional tips:

- Ask the same base questions of all candidates for the same job.

- Avoid any question or line of questioning that could focus on a person's protected class as defined under local, state, and federal regulations (https://www.eeoc.gov/employers/small-business/3-who-protected-employment-discrimination).

- If an employee volunteers information that would be considered protected information under these regulations, it is best to simply put your pen down, listen, and move on. Don't probe further. By putting your pen down, the candidate will see that you have not recorded any information that may be used later in the hiring decision.

- Seek feedback from others in the interview process and ensure they are following the same guidance as above. Align ahead of time who will focus on what questions.

- Document your final decision, including feedback received from each interviewer, in a consistent manner focusing on qualifications and capabilities.

Consistency is key. You will do well if you and the other interviewers have treated each candidate consistently. You can honestly show that the ultimate hiring decision was based on the job requirements and not on other non-defensible/protected characteristics of the candidate.

Chapter 4

Retain or Release

In fact, whoever is moving the slowest in the [team] is the one who will govern throughput.[6]

Sam was not cutting it.

The team needed to pick up the pace of work and keep the quality high. Sam had come into the team at a slow time. As the work and projects picked up, other team members rose to the challenge, but Sam's team leaders and manager observed that he seemed stuck. And the manager had spoken to Sam about this before.

The situation was causing a disruption in the team. Everyone needed to pull his or her own weight, but other members were having to clean up Sam's work. This was causing a serious risk to other projects and deliverables. Prior to meeting with Sam to discuss the issues and need for correction, the manager sought counsel from HR.

Sam's manager set up a meeting, spelled out the facts, and outlined the problems. He reminded Sam of their previous discussions on these concerns. These were causing a significant strain on the rest of the team and the overall performance and reputation of the department. The manager probed further on how Sam felt the current job aligned with his strengths and what additional resources he needed in order to succeed. Sam said he understood and was trying his best.

Sam was to be given a special project, access to the people and tools he needed, and agreed to weekly touch-point meetings. His manager asked him to reflect on this feedback and proposed project. Then, the manager scheduled to meet with him the next day so that Sam could present his proposed action plan. They also discussed other support Sam might need. The manager told Sam that he wanted him to succeed and said he would be available anytime Sam needed input, even in addition to the weekly touch points. Sam's action plan, along with his manager's contributions, became the basis of the Performance Improvement Plan (often referred to as a PIP). Sam reiterated his desire to make the necessary improvements and felt confident he could do so. His manager documented this in writing. He restated the serious nature of this performance improvement plan. If there was no significant improvement, other consequences, including Sam's release, would be considered.

Hit the Pause Button

As a creative person who is new to management, this may feel overwhelming at first, so let's review the steps that were involved to get to this point.

1. The manager observed performance issues and quickly took steps to address them.
2. The manager gathered the facts before meeting with the employee.
3. The manager arranged for a private meeting with the employee and covered the following:

WHAT the purpose of the meeting was and what were the performance issues that needed to be addressed?

- Be clear about the facts. Remind the employee of past conversations and summarize the issues clearly and concisely.

WHY are the performance issues a problem?

- So often, as managers, we can articulate what the problem is but fail to help the employee understand the "why." Helping the employee see the direct impact on the team, department, or company performance goes a long way in motivating the employee to correct the situation.

HOW is the employee going to make the necessary corrections?

- Instead of coming into the meeting with all the answers, ask the employee to create a plan to address the issues. Together, agree on a suitable action plan, including what the agreed upon outcomes and timeline will be. The employee is more likely to achieve solutions they had a hand in creating than simply a list of directives handed down by the manager. Depending on the complexity or emotions of hearing the earlier WHAT and WHY feedback, it is best to schedule a follow-up meeting so the employee can present a well thought out plan. With the emotions removed, the manager and employee can have a productive dialogue including what other support, training, or resources the employee will need to ensure a successful outcome.

WHEN will the employee meet to touch base with the manager, and how much time will be suitable to demonstrate consistent improvement?

- Ask the employee to schedule regular touch-base meetings and hold them accountable to do so. Again, the more the employee owns their improvement plan, the more likely you will see a successful outcome. Let's pause here on the last part of the "when" question. You may have heard reference to a ninety-day performance improvement plan. While that is likely a suitable period to show sufficient and sustained performance improvement, you do not want to get locked into a fixed period. You will want to adjust the time period to fit the performance or behavior change needed. What if the issue is more behavioral (e.g. violation of company directive or policy, habitual attendance issues, etc.)? You are not going to give someone ninety days to follow a policy; it should be followed immediately. And if the employee chooses not to make the change, then move to the immediate consequences, including termination, depending on the severity of the infraction.

- The manager closes the meeting by reiterating confidence and value in the employee. The manager also must be clear about the seriousness of the PIP and what the possible consequences are if there is not sufficient progress or results as outlined in the PIP. If this is not the first time the manager has had to address the employee on these performance concerns, the manager should be clear that termination may need to be considered.

- The manager creates the final performance improvement plan (PIP) using both the employee's proposed actions along with agreed upon expectations and support needed—as discussed in the meeting. Many companies will have a prescribed format to be used and require the employee and manager to sign the document and return to HR for placement in the employee's personnel file. Absent of this, an email may serve as an equally reliable form of documentation. Throughout this performance improvement period, the manager should send summary emails after each touch-base meeting to confirm progress or other agreements. A summary email should only be used to summarize an actual meeting and not to replace one.

Back to Sam's Story

At two weeks into the PIP, Sam's manager noticed that Sam was not taking direction well and spent time focusing on the wrong parts of the project. He sometimes jumped ahead, circumventing the process to discern the best solution. His manager also received feedback from other team leads that Sam was not reaching out to peers or leadership for feedback except at the weekly team meetings. When given direction, Sam would either ignore it or forget it and continue in his own direction.

I met with Sam after one of the touch-point meetings and shared my observations.

"Sam, I don't see you taking notes during the meetings. I understand not everyone is a note-taker, but when you miss feedback and directions, leadership wonders if you're paying attention."

"Yeah, I know," Sam said. "I'll do better next time."

"Sam, before the next team meeting, please connect with me or the other team leads to discuss your ideas and show your work. I am happy to give you feedback and connect you with people and research if you need it."

"Thanks, I appreciate that. I'll definitely reach out."

And Sam did reach out over the following two weeks, but after that he dropped back into his old habits. By this time, the agreed upon performance improvement plan was almost half over, and key deadlines had been missed. Sam's manager was getting concerned about the lack of change and moved quickly to address this with Sam. The manager met with Sam to provide clear feedback with examples related to the lack of progress and missed deadlines. He reiterated the seriousness of the situation and reminded Sam again of the agreed upon plan and consequences. The manager asked Sam what specific steps he would take to get back on track. Sam agreed with the feedback and agreed he would do better, but he did not provide any details in terms of concrete actions. The manager sent an email following the meeting to Sam summarizing the meeting and asked that Sam reply back his understanding.

In the end, Sam was not able to make the necessary changes and did not meet the outcome expectations. The manager, in consultation with HR, decided it was best to release, or terminate, him. Sam was not surprised. He knew he was struggling to meet these expectations and later admitted to a co-worker that he was relieved to be able to move on to new opportunities.

Contrast this with Ani.

Ani had been in a similar situation. Although she had been with the team for years, once the pace started to pick up, Ani found herself struggling.

It is worth noting at this point that creative people can often fall into a rut in how they think and approach work. Creative people like to innovate fresh ideas and solutions. If work is slow, creatives can fall into a lull that is hard to get out of by themselves. They often need to be roused out of their mental lethargy. While some creatives have been exposed to formal, rigorous training, and developing new ways of problem solving, others have organically learned a few techniques to get by with and fall back on when under pressure. Some from this latter group have the talent to learn and grow but lack motivation. They too need a wake-up call to spur them on to greater heights.

Ani was just such a person. After embarking on the performance improvement plan, or PIP as noted above, Ani was spurred into action. It was not easy for her, but she rose to the occasion and, in the end, she excelled. She knew the facts and faced them. She knew the outcome and was willing to do what it took to retain her job. Plus, her manager retained a valuable and talented employee.

So What Was the Difference?

Was it a difference in temperaments between these two creatives? Was it a difference in work styles or attitudes? It is likely these were contributing factors. Both were provided the observations and facts about their work's impact on the work of the team. Both were given a plan for success and the resources and time needed to achieve the performance improvement plan. Both had regular feedback and knew where they stood in regard to the PIP. The final decision to retain or release should not have been a surprise. Each person was treated professionally with respect, dignity, and care. Remove the emotion and use facts. Dismissal should NEVER be a surprise.

Is Releasing an Employee Tough?

Sure, it is if you care about people. Is it necessary? Absolutely. In light of the impact to the larger team, your job is to ensure you hire and retain the best talent and release those who are not. Is there a happy ending? That depends on each person. I have talked to people fired from positions after a lengthy process of trying to sincerely help them succeed. Some have thanked me afterward. They needed a kick in the pants to get moving and realize their own potential. Others are still wallowing in the mire of self-pity and doubt. Ultimately, it is up to them how they choose to respond. There is no one answer to all the possible situations. The two examples above give you a baseline in terms of approach. It is critical that you gain feedback from trusted partners in your organization—your manager and HR. They can be invaluable in discussing your concerns and provide time-tested advice on the best approach that fits the situation. Leading people and navigating the potential legal minefields can feel overwhelming. Don't let it discourage you or, more importantly, delay your action. Provide clear and consistent expectations and regular and timely feedback. Offer support and a listening ear. Be the kind of leader you wish you had.

Advice from Human Resources

Meet with HR to understand your organization's approach to performance management. Due to legal requirements, most methods will be the same. Yet processes and procedures can vary from company to company.

Whew! That is a lot to absorb for Week 1. Let's begin to apply what you have learned.

Applications for Week 1

We have covered a lot this week. Below is a list of actions you will apply to get to know your team better. These will take time. How much time is up to you. Be willing and intentional about setting time aside to complete this list. Also, try your best to connect with HR and be a partner. You'll be setting yourself up for the next week as you go.

Practical Applications

Okay, here are our first applications. Let's get started.

1. Calendar initial meetings to hear employee stories.
2. Take the temperament assessment.
3. Have each team member take the temperament assessment.
4. Create a team temperament grid.

Calendar Meetings with Each Employee

Calendar meetings to hear employee stories. Spend time with each of them. Get to know their background stories, their hard and soft skills, their likes and dislikes, and their goals. Write these things down. You will begin creating a Team Profile Sheet (TPS). You can do this in a notebook or use the *Creatives Lead Companion Workbook.*

- Practice empathy by putting yourself in their shoes.
- How would you want to be treated?

Take the Temperament Assessment

If you haven't already, take the temperament assessment (see link below). This online assessment should take no more than five to ten minutes to complete. You can find it here by visiting: http://bit.ly/3bicte9

Team Member Assessments

Ask each of your team members to take the assessment and share their results with you. You will use their results to fill in a team grid. This will help you learn about the team makeup and how to better resource and communicate with them.

Create a Temperaments Grid

Put together the temperament grid, and list your team's primary and secondary results. You'll use this for yourself and the upcoming team off-site meeting.

Example: Primary Temperaments

Entertainer	Entrepreneur
Tom	Erin
Sammy	Sam
Gamer	**Architect**
Bill	Beth
Rashid	Andrew
Timothy	

Example: Secondary Temperaments

Entertainer	Entrepreneur
Tom	Beth
Sam	Sammy
Bill	
Gamer	**Architect**
Andrew	Erin
	Rashid
	Timothy

Look People in the Eye

Building trust is tantamount to creating a high-performing team. Show respect, competence, and that you care about your team.

- Show Respect
- Show You Care
- 5 Keys to Competence
- Week 2 Practical Applications

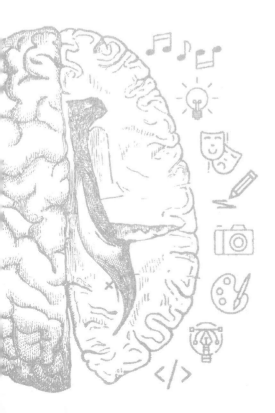

Creatives Lead

Chapter 5
Show Respect

Xavier had been working hard all month. He had taken on several new projects that were stretching his capacity, but he had a hard time saying "no" to interesting work. Not only had he been working on the magazine design, but he was also doing several mailers, custom designs for a series of audio messages, and had been learning 3D animation to fill in for another employee who was on an extended leave of absence.

He enjoyed the variety of work and the ability to bring his training and expertise to these projects. He prided himself on staying abreast of the design styles and trends in the industry. Is it any wonder he got upset after his new boss, Jim, came to him and began making creative changes to the projects based on his personal likes/dislikes? And, to top it off, instead of respecting Xavier and thanking him for taking on the extra work, Jim harped on Xavier's one missed deadline for the whole year.

"Who needs this?" Xavier said to himself. "And Jim's not even a designer; he's a marketing guy!"

Because they are creative people, your employees take a unique pride in their work and often feel like they have invested a piece of themselves in the work. As a new leader, you need to remember what it was like when you first hired. You were a specialist that had honed your craft. Your training and expertise made you valuable. You wanted respect for your design skills and the experiences you brought to the organization. Your employees want the same thing.

Appreciate People

Appreciate the people who work *with* and *for* you. A reputable leader shows appreciation for his employees but also for his business partners—those who work in concert with him but, are not direct reports. Appreciation can be communicated through words like:

"Thanks for all your hard work!"

"You're a great partner."

"I appreciate your skills and the contributions you make to the team."

And actions like:

- Bringing in healthy snacks for the team.
- Taking the team out for a movie or game of laser tag.
- Telling folks to leave an hour early.
- A hand-written thank you note.
- Providing lunch for a partnering team.

Another way to show appreciation is to jump into the work where you can help out most. Nothing speaks louder than when your team sees you, the leader, pitching in to help through crunch times. Some could take this the wrong way and feel that they are not up to the job. Here, you can sincerely acknowledge that having limitations does not mean they or their skills are inferior. As a team, you work together.

Acknowledge People

Showing respect to your team also means to accept them and their differences. Every creative person is different and expresses themselves in distinct ways. Acknowledge the fact that people have different backgrounds, learning styles, and ways of presenting themselves.

Allow for the myriad of learning styles your team may have. When you meet, mentor, and instruct, take into consideration these seven learning styles:[7]

- **Visual** (spatial): They prefer using pictures, images, and spatial understanding.
- **Aural** (auditory-musical): They prefer using sound and music.
- **Verbal** (linguistic): They prefer using words, both in speech and writing.
- **Physical** (kinesthetic): They prefer using their body, hands, and sense of touch.
- **Logical** (mathematical): They prefer using logic, reasoning, and systems.
- **Social** (interpersonal): They prefer to learn in groups or with other people.
- **Solitary** (intrapersonal): They prefer to work alone and use self study.

Acknowledge your people by allowing them to present themselves in self-expressive ways that are appropriate for your place of business. Coming from a creative background, you know how that can look—toys and mementos on the desk; decorating their cubicle in themes; wearing fun socks; wearing hats; facial hair; multi-colored hair. Allow the creative people to be creative. Take a look at what Pixar® and Zappos® employees have done to make their spaces their own and show their personal creative flair. Simply search online images for either "pixar cubicles" or "zappos cubicles" and enjoy the inspiration.

Chapter 6
Show You Care

"Hey Al, how is your mother doing?" I asked.

Al looked up quizzically. "You remember my mom? Wow. She is doing much better. Thanks for asking."

"How was your vacation, Sarah?"

"It was amazing! I took so many pictures."

"Wonderful!" I exclaimed. "I would love to see some if you'd like to share."

"What are you learning in your workshop, Ben?"

"I am learning so much! I cannot wait to put some of it into practice with some of my projects."

"Me either. Would you be willing to share what you're learning with other members of the team?"

"Sure!" Ben said. "I have already been talking about it to some of my lunch buddies."

"June, I am so sorry to hear about your uncle's death. I am going to bring over a homemade meal tonight. Is that okay?"

"You don't have to do that," June said.

"I know, but I want to. Does your family like beef tenderloin, buttermilk mashed potatoes, and Green Beans Almondine?"

"Yeah! My kids will love that."

Team members used to laugh at me because I carried a large DayTimer®. "Dang, Eric, you can use that as a weapon!" they would jokingly say. What they did not know was the amount of notes I kept. Any time we were in a meeting, and an employee would share a concern or exciting news, I would write it down. Why? Because I cared about the team members. I wanted to remember their concerns and excitement. I wanted to follow up during one-on-one meetings to see how I could help them. I wish I could say everything was committed to memory, but it was not. I had too much I was responsible for, but I knew I wanted to remember these kinds of events, so I wrote them down.

Know What is Going on with Your People

It may becoming clear that leadership has challenges. You too have a boss who is expecting you and the team to produce excellent work in a timely fashion. You have employees who look to you for challenging projects and fair compensation. You are also trying to balance your new role while motivating a variety of unique personalities and creative skill sets.

A good leader will know what's going on in their employees' lives and in the workplace. For example, you can acknowledge the need of a parent of three to stay home with sick children, while also recognizing that the single colleague shouldn't always have to stay late because they don't have a family to rush home to.

So how does this work out practically? Well, it depends. It depends on how you entered this role. Were you promoted up from within the department? Were you promoted up from within the organization? Were you hired from the outside? Let's take a look at each scenario.

Promoted From Within the Department

You likely know and have worked with the employees you will be leading. They have been your friends and teammates. You already know a lot about them, and they know a lot about you. How do they feel about you now? Did any of them get passed up as a result of your promotion? One of the biggest hurdles you will face is overcoming the "buddy" relationship.

The challenge comes when you have urgent deadlines or when a friend takes advantage of your previous relationship and assumes it's okay to come in late. This is where a line needs to be drawn. Author and founder of Fox and Company, Jefferey Fox, said it best in his book, *How to Become a Great Boss*, "employees want a boss, not a buddy."[8] This doesn't mean being "bossy", but it does mean your previous relationship *has* to change. To keep from hurt feelings and misunderstandings, you need to set expectations early. You will need to modify what you share and how you share it. You will be held to a higher standard by your peers, and those are the new relationships you need to cultivate. Navigating these waters can be tricky, but they can be done.

Promoted From Within the Organization

You will likely not know the people you will be leading. But you will be bringing a reputation. Do you know what that reputation is? Have you led creative people before? If not, you will have a challenge earning "street cred" and respect. Creative teams will have a hard time trusting you and your opinion.

Meeting the team one-on-one will help you to establish a rapport (see Week 1 Practical Application). Setting expectations early will also help. The *biggest* help will be for you to admit your knowledge gaps, let the team know you are working on those gaps, and let the team know you are *trusting them* and their expertise to get the job done.

Hired From the Outside

You have come from a different culture. You have come from a different team—a team that you likely crafted into a smooth-running engine. Now you have been placed over a team in a "new garage", and the "engine" may need a tune-up or an overhaul. You need to find out quickly.

Don't be too quick to implement what worked for you in the past. It's in the past, and this is the present—in a new company with different values. Get to know your leadership peers and the nuances of your role in this fresh environment. Learn about the team and unique culture norms before you rush out your novel ideas and ways of doing work.

Encourage People

A good leader encourages her people in numerous ways. Verbal and nonverbal, in public and in private are all ways to encourage people. The goal is to be intentional, timely, and consistent.

Tell people in your one-on-one meetings what you have seen them doing that promotes a healthy environment. When called for, praise your people in public settings to let them know you care, you're watching, and you're aware of their valuable contributions.

Nonverbal ways to show you care are individual cards (yes, this means handwritten notes), email messages, and text messages. If you have a food budget, picking up healthy snacks, breakfast treats, or taking the team out for lunch or happy hour are additional ways to show you care. When I didn't have a budget, I'd pay for some of these out of my own pocket because that's how much it meant to me. It also means a lot to your people!

Develop People

A good leader will recognize that employees want to better themselves and further their careers. They should not be threatened by this. Good managers will help find professional development opportunities and allow employees to take part in new projects when it is applicable to their talents, time, and goals.

Sit down in your one-on-ones and set career goals. Many creative people want to excel at their craft and learn new tools, trends, and techniques. Invest in them, and they will invest in you.

If you see or get feedback about team members displaying poor performance like needing to work faster, solving for multiple iterations, learning empathy, or time management—make recommendations to them. Help them develop a plan and set expectations for achieving the plan.

The bottom line: get to know people. Get to know the dynamics of the team. Get to know your peers. Get to know the cultural nuances in your role. All of these exercises will build your confidence and the confidence of your people as a leader who cares.

Chapter 7

5 Keys to Competence

Deena was frustrated. She had a new manager who had moved over to fill a leadership role within the organization. That in itself wasn't so bad except this leader came from the finance department and knew absolutely nothing about the web, web users, web design, or usability.

"He doesn't know web design, interaction design, communication, or user experience research. He asked me to make changes to our web page based on his mother's tiny monitor that she has at home!"

"Give him some room to grow," I encouraged her. "You can use this time to help him learn about web design and establish yourself as the expert."

"I know, it's just so hard to think he's supposed to represent our team in leadership meetings, when he doesn't even know what we do or how it gets done!"

I have heard stories like Deena's for years. Creatives have a hard time respecting leaders who do not show any competence in the creative process or understand the expertise of their craft.

Having come from a creative background, this should not be a big issue for you. One of the best things you can do is admit your weaknesses to your team, recognize their expertise, and share your willingness to learn. Author and coach Dan Miller offers these often overlooked factors that can become the keys to success in all you do.[9] I hope you find them as informative and applicable as I did.

The Five Keys

1. Passion

Without passion, a person drifts aimlessly through life taking each event and day as it comes—firefighting and rolling with the punches from week to week. But a person with passion is a person with goals. He has a target, and he is on the road to achievement.

Questions:

- What are your short-term goals as a new leader?
- What are the goals for your team over the next three to six months?
- What are the goals for the work you are doing over the next six to nine months?

2. Determination

Many leaders talk about purpose—having a purpose in life and a purpose for the things they do on a daily basis. When there is a purpose, there is determination to see it through. If an obstacle arises, it does not send a person spinning into other directions. An on-purpose person has the determination to stick it out and work through the obstacle to keep moving toward his goal.

Questions:

- What current obstacles are you facing?
- Why might you be thinking of backing down from a hurdle or goal?
- What will it take for you to move ahead?
- Who can you talk to for help with your obstacles and goals?

3. Self-Discipline

Many dislike this word because discipline does not come naturally to us. I struggle with this as well, but without self-discipline a person can be easily swayed. This is often the foundational character quality that the other keys are built upon.

Questions:

- What comes to mind when you think of self-discipline?
- How does self-discipline, or lack thereof, impact your life?
- In what area(s) of your work and/or personal life do you lack discipline?
- How can you invite others to hold you accountable?

4. Talent

There are a lot of books today about talent. Finding your unique talent and strengths makes you a better employee and person. As Jim Collins said in his book *Good to Great* and Marcus Buckingham said in his books, *First Break All The Rules* and *Now Discover Your Strengths,* not everyone is talented in *every* area. Yet, everyone has a talent. Wise is the person who discovers his talent and maximizes it.

Questions:

- Have you discovered your talent(s)?
- What can you do to maximize your talents?
- How can you make sure your weaknesses are compensated for?
- What are the talents of your team members?
- Are they aligned to maximize their talents and minimize their weaknesses?

5. Faith

You have done your research, you have crunched the numbers, you have talked with various people you trust, but there is still the uncertainty of the unknown. This is where faith comes into play. Sometimes you just have to step out. You cannot reach new heights by having both feet on the ground.

Questions:

- Would you consider yourself a person of faith?

- What or who is your faith in?

- How does faith impact how you handle stress?

- How does your decision-making align with your faith?

Your team wants a person who they feel is competent. They will appreciate you being up-front with them about not only your strengths but weaknesses as well. It will give them a confidence and trust in you as a leader and how you buffer and represent them with other leaders. Applying the five keys will propel you forward. Take time at the end of this reading to reflect on the questions above. Write down what you *have* learned and what you *need* to learn to become the competent leader your team needs.

Applications for Week 2

This week you've explored respect, competence, and care as themes. Now it's time to put them into practice.

Practical Applications

This week there are a lot of meetings for you to schedule. These meetings might look like too much at first. You will be setting a weekly cadence with team members. This practice will soon become second nature.

1. Calendar one-on-one meetings.
2. Begin setting expectations.
3. Look for ways to encourage and recognize people.
4. Set aside time to get to know your peers and the nuances of your new role.
5. Schedule your strategic off-site meeting two to three weeks out, to discuss long-term goals. I find a Monday or Friday works best.

Calendar, Goals, and Setting Meetings

Put meetings on the calendar to set personal and professional goals. Team members don't care how much you know until they know how much you care. Ask each team member to begin working on a *Career Development Plan* (CDP). Let the team members know you are "on their side" and want to see them succeed. Check with HR to see if they have a CDP process set up.

Begin to Set Clear Expectations

Setting clear expectations for performance is something you want to start early (more in Week 3). You can begin during the one-on-one meetings and discuss further in team meetings.

Ways to Recognize People

Inspire employees to a higher standard. Look for opportunities to encourage and recognize people when you catch them doing the things that enforce positive culture. You'll find what gets rewarded gets repeated. Be sure to align the recognition to each person's preference (e.g. some like individual words of affirmation, while others like to be recognized in front of the team). See the list below for a few ideas and suggestions.

- Comments
- Cards and Emails
- Social Media shout-outs (Check with HR)
- 1-on-1 lunch
- Public accolades (know each person—if they are introverted, they may feel uncomfortable with public recognition)
- Birthday cake or card
- Work Anniversaries
- Does your company offer financial rewards?

Check with your HR department to make sure what you can and cannot do when it comes to recognizing employees.

Get to Know Your Peers

You are the new kid on the block. You may have peers you work with directly or indirectly. Set up time with each to get to know them and how you can support them. Use this time to begin to build bridges and to learn the subtle distinctions of your role. Your peers can be a great source of information and inspiration.

Schedule the Strategic Off-Site

Don't sweat the details yet. I will provide you with tools over the next couple weeks. But be sure to schedule this on the team calendar as a place holder. People can block out the time if they know it is coming. If the team asks for additional information, let them know it will be coming shortly along with an agenda and any pre-event preparations.

Use Your Words

This is a big week! Communication is key. You'll prepare for your strategic team off-site meeting. There, you will be reinforcing expectations, the importance of communication, and accountability for the months ahead.

- Leadership Lesson from Little League
- Communicate, Communicate
- Misunderstandings
- Week 3 Practical Applications

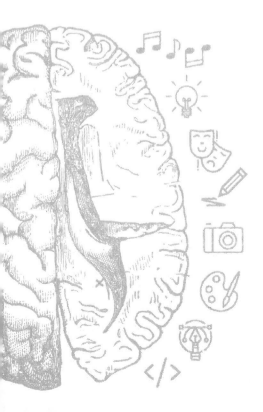

Chapter 8

A Leadership Lesson from Little League

"My name is Coach Brown. Welcome to Little League baseball. I expect you to be at practice on time with your gear. I expect you to practice with one of your parents when you're at home, to study hard in school, and to play the positions I assign you to. I also expect you to listen to me and Coach Bath and, above all, to have fun. I can tell this is going to be an awesome team! Do you have any questions for me before we get started?"

"Coach Brown?"

"Yes?"

"How tall are you?"

"I am six foot seven."

And that's the way Little League started.

If you're familiar with *First, Break All The Rules: What the World's Greatest Managers Do Differently* by Marcus Buckingham and Jim Harter, you may recall the section about great managers not spending a lot of time with their poor performers. The idea being extolled here is that if you work with your star performers, you and the company will benefit more than wasting time and energy with their poorer counterparts. There is certainly some truth to this concept, and it has been played out in businesses all around the world. While I would not totally disagree, I have learned that some people just need a little push of encouragement.

Years ago, as I coached my son's baseball team, there were some poor performers on the team. At the time I wondered, "Should I not spend much time with them? I have several players that are very good for their age. Should I focus more time with them?" Some business gurus would have answered, "Yes."

Before you discount this chapter, read on.

Expectation setting is a common practice within business. It brings clarity to the team. Communicating to your team as a whole and with the individual members is essential. Yet, I want to add another idea to expectation setting—aspiration setting. People want to aspire to something greater. We have all had those moments in life when someone spoke into us a vision for what we could become. You will want to do this for your team.

Defining Moments

Think back to when you were on a sports team, or in school, or starting your first creative job. You were a little clumsy, maybe shy or awkward—definitely nervous. Then along came this coach/teacher/boss whom you will never forget. They saw something in you that others did not. He or she encouraged you by spending time with you and telling you that there were big things ahead for you. You latched onto those words and never forgot. To this day, you count that as a defining moment. A time that someone, whose power and authority you were under, gave you the nudge you needed to get rolling. Some of you have even had the chance to tell that person how much that meant to you and that you wouldn't be where you are now if it were not for that moment in time. Some of you wish you could tell that special person how much they meant to you, but time and distance have gotten in the way, and you've lost touch with them.

A Little Push Can Start the Engine

Don't chalk this chapter up to a feel-good story. I have seen how an encouraging word fires up a person and gets his or her self-confidence engine running. I have seen it in the workplace. I have personally experienced it when I was a college student. And I saw it each week on the baseball field as those little guys came out to practice.

Back to my question: Should I not spend time with the poor performers and focus more on the star performers on the team?

I say, "Yes and no."

Your objective as a leader is to provide coaching. This involves feedback, direction, and encouragement. You have no idea how your words affect the team on a weekly basis. Wait, let me rephrase that. The reality is, you *need to know* that what you say affects the team.

There is a very real, practical, and powerful principle at work here. The power of words. Words spoken in ways that can build up and not tear down. Words that can inspire and not demoralize.

Those of us in positions of influence and authority can wield words like a healing balm or a wounding sword. You—as a boss, parent, teacher, coach, and trusted advisor—need to take heed. You need to clearly set your expectations for the team, *and* you need to inspire the team. Spend a little extra time with your weaker performers. Encourage them and speak words of life into them. And, one day, like the character Richard Dreyfuss played in the movie, *Mr. Holland's Opus* (one of my favorites), you may find yourself the center of admiration for a new generation of leaders.

Chapter 9

Communicate, Communicate

After completing a contract job with a Fortune 500 company, I asked to have a "post mortem" meeting—you know, after a project is complete you review pros and cons of how the project went in order to improve the next go-around. During this meeting, communication styles, expectations on frequency, best methods for communication, and availability to communicate were the topics of the conversation. Communication is a *big deal!* Yet, it continues to amaze me that all around the world we "flap our lips" every day in verbal communication, but are we truly understanding each other?

Effective communication is not natural to us. It is something we need to work on every day. Yet, because we "talk" every day, we do not feel the need to work on improving this area. Like our temperaments, the tendency is to converse and share information in a way that is familiar to us. We expect it to be the same with those with whom we interact. Take heart. Although effective communication does not come naturally, it is a skill that can be learned.

Your Communication Language

Ever hear of the *The 5 Love Languages,* authored by Gary Chapman? He presents the idea that people express love in *their love language* and expect the same language in return. Yet, those close to you often have a differing love language, and therein lies the issue of unmet expectations, frustrations, and lack of intimacy. Much like love languages, there are communication languages—how you prefer to communicate and receive communication in return. To be effective, you need to know yours and the languages of those to whom you are communicating. The three categories I have broken these into are nonverbal media, verbal media, and face to face.

Nonverbal Media

Texting/Notes

For people who like texting, short bursts of nonverbal communication are preferred. It is often top-of-mind information and, in our smart-device dependent world, it's also attention-getting. Leaving sticky notes on the counter, fridge, or computer monitor is another way this kind of person likes to communicate. There are pros (attention-getting, to the point, automatic records with message threads) and cons (typos, no verbal nuances or facial cues, misunderstandings, little context) to this method. If this is your preferred language, be sure to communicate it to those around you so they know how best to reach you or get your attention on a subject. If texting is your personal preference, you may want to set boundaries around the kinds of messages you see as appropriate (e.g. "I am running late" or "Let's talk later"). You will likely discourage off-hours texting as well, unless there is an emergency.

Email/Letters

For others, a lengthier email or handwritten letter is preferred. These should provide more context than short-burst communications. If you feel you're reading or writing a book, you should opt for a verbal style—no one likes to read lengthy emails. Here too are pros (more context, automated message threads, greater detail) and cons (typos, misunderstandings, lack of physical cues). Use language judiciously for the information you are trying to communicate.

Verbal Media

Phone/Audio

If you tend to be a "talker" or verbal processor, the phone or other audio languages will likely be your preference. You are bothered by the distraction of text messages and rarely read email. You want to get to the point quickly and solve problems without waiting for the back-and-forth of email or texting. Some of the pros are real-time dialog and clarifying misunderstandings. Some of the cons are lack of availability, leaving messages, and no nonverbal observations. If this is your language, let your team and friends know.

Video

Video conferencing is a step toward a more holistic communication language. It has all the benefits of phone/audio as well as allowing others to see you and your facial reactions. The downsides to video conferencing are low bandwidth pauses and skips in the conversation. Sometimes the service will "kick you out," and sometimes the other parties may not turn on or have the capability to show video of themselves. All this can feel like a disjointed conversation and leave you less than satisfied.

Face to Face

Finally, we get to good old fashioned face-to-face, in-the-same-room communication. This is by far the richest form of communication, but in our global economy, can be easily discarded for a previously mentioned media of choice. Having met face to face with company leaders from various countries, I can tell you face to face communication shaved weeks off back-and-forth clarifying, confirming, and confusion. It has allowed me to build trust as well as better working relationships. Is face to face hard? You bet it is—especially if you are introverted, but that is not an excuse to sideline this communication style. It has all the pros with what some may say is a con of cost. I can tell you, the cost and time requirements are higher if you're not getting your people together. This communication style can minimize weeks of back and forth and maximize clarity and details. Finally, face-to-face is the best style for communicating negative or difficult information. The phone would be the best second option only if face to face cannot be achieved.

Summing It Up

In our fast-paced world, clear and effective communication is a must. We live or die by how well we communicate. Depending on your environment, communication can take several forms: verbal, nonverbal, email, phone, memos and letters, instant messaging, text messaging, video conferencing, social media, and more. Personal preferences, cultural differences, and accessibility all factor into good communication. Communicating takes work, and those who are wise will invest the time and energy to make this an everyday priority. Your work, your relationships, your family, and your very life may depend on it.

Counterintuitively, a main ingredient of communication is silence and listening. It should be noted, there is a difference between hearing and listening. Hearing is biological while listening is learned behavior. This is almost always ignored. We all have *something* to say. When others are talking to us, instead of listening we're thinking of what we want to say next.

Ever been guilty of that?

In closing this chapter, I have listed below principles for incredible communication through listening. I know it is hard, but avoid the temptation to interrupt and use the principles here:

Listening with Your Eyes

Often, body language communicates more than words. Look at your body language as well as the person you're talking with. Also, look into the eyes of the person. Do not look at other things around you—this communicates you're not attentive, interested, or respecting what the other person is saying.

Listening with Your Ears

Focus on what the other person is saying by giving your *full* attention. Don't get distracted by thinking of your response while the other person is talking. Don't talk back, although asking some probing questions may be relevant to get clarity (it also lets the other person know that you *are* listening).

Listening with Your Feelings

Try as best you can to "read between the lines" of what the other person is saying. Look to understand their feelings about the topic. As Stephen R. Covey said, "Seek to understand before being understood."

For more on effective communication, see:

- *The Time Trap* by Alec Mackenzie, see section two: Biggest Time Wasters – Poor Communication.

- *What Every Body Is Saying: An Ex-FBI Agent's Guide to Speed-Reading People,* by Joe Navarro and Marvin Karlins about interpreting body language.

- *The 5 Languages of Appreciation in the Workplace: Empowering Organizations by Encouraging People* by Gary Chapman and Paul White.

Creatives Lead

Chapter 10
Expectations

Everyone has expectations.

You have expectations of your team, and your team has expectations of you. Your boss has expectations of you, and you have expectations of her. Your peers also have expectations of you. You have expectations of *you*, and the list goes on.

What is the one issue that causes the most frustration, hurt, anger, and misunderstanding in all relationships, whether work-related or personal?

Unmet expectations.

Have you been to a networking, company, or neighborhood event and felt that everyone you met expected something from you? You leave thinking, "I thought this was a relationship-building occasion, not a sell-yourself meeting." If a person didn't show interest in who you were or what you had to offer as a person, they had no time for you and moved on to the next "business opportunity."

How do you feel coming from these events? Do you feel understood for who you are and what you have to offer as a person, peer, boss, or co-worker? How do you think your team feels coming away from conversations with you? Instead of wanting something *from* the people you interact with—how about wanting something *for* them?

Does this concept seem upside down to you?

Why is it we expect people to treat us with respect and show interest in us when we do not reciprocate? Do we talk to people to broadcast or to honestly communicate? Is it truly a dialogue, or do you often find yourself in a monologue? This tells something about our motivation, doesn't it?

So what are we to do? Certainly, we want communication to be worth our time and effort. We want to communicate our expectations and mitigate misunderstandings—right?

I recommend a relational approach. Be *genuinely* interested in others first. Find out what they do and how you can help them succeed. Anne Baber and Lynne Waymon offer several excellent suggestions in their book, *Make Your Contacts Count*. While their book is primarily about creating a contact network, the principles apply to relationship building. Above all, you want to communicate your expectations and that you can be trusted by letting people see your *character* and your *competence*.[10]

Character

- Be unfailingly reliable.
- Do what you say you will when you say you will.
- Be willing to be held accountable.
- Voice your expectations regularly.
- Meet deadlines.
- Go for the win/win solution.
- Treat everyone you meet fairly.
- Speak well of people even when they are not present.
- Collaborate rather than compete.
- When something goes wrong, make it right.
- Compensate generously for your failure.
- Go the extra mile.
- Respect other people's time and possessions.

Competency

- Earn the proper credentials.
- Stay at the leading edge of your profession and craft.

- Win praise and awards from your peers.
- Take lifelong learning seriously.
- Teach or mentor others.
- Consult with others to share expertise.
- Do the job right the first time.
- Handle the "little stuff" with care.
- Follow through to make sure you meet or exceed expectations.

Early and Often

We started by discussing expectations. Many issues arise because expectations are either not voiced or not clearly defined, causing misunderstandings, incomplete work, poor communication, and hurt feelings. Don't wait until things get bad or projects are running late before you start addressing expectations. Communicating your expectations early and often is the sign of a good leader.

If you approach communication, expectation setting, and accountability as a means to building relationships, you are headed in a successful leadership direction. Over time, you will have numerous relationships that will pay big dividends in the end. You will experience a good reputation—one who can be trusted, can get the job done, and is looking out for the success of those around her.

Creatives Lead

Applications for Week 3

Setting clear expectations, communication, and accountability is what you are planning for as you head into your strategic off-site.

Practical Applications

Only two items to work on this week:

1. Plan and prepare for your strategic off-site.
2. Use the template and resources provided.

Prepare the Strategic Off-site

Plan and prepare your strategic off-site. You should have one to two weeks to pull your material together for:

- Team building
- Communicating and expectations
- Socializing
- Reviewing data
- Setting strategic goals for 6-12 months ahead

Template and Resources

Use my sample template with agenda, exercises, and items to review for your off-site. Think of it as an idea starter and make it your own. You should give it a theme to make it feel more fun. This one uses a baseball theme.

Here is a template for the strategic off-site: http://bit.ly/3jL01Gp

- It is critical to set up this meeting and gather your information ahead of time.

- Be prepared to put together a PowerPoint or Keynote presentation.

- Get away from the office or your day-in-day-out surroundings. This helps limit mental distractions.

- Allow ample time for lunch together and team bonding.

- If you have inspirational or industry articles, you can send those out ahead as a pre-read and then discuss during your time together.

- Be sure to end on a high note or invite the team to finish the day at a happy hour in another location.

If face-to-face is not an option, you should video conference. Seeing each other is critical to the success of an off-site meeting for team building. Here are some tips for a successful virtual planning meeting:

- Conduct over one to two full days or three half days if necessary.

- Divide the day into 90-minute chunks/sessions.

- Allow for a 10-15 minute break after each chunk (gives people a break from sitting and staring at a screen too long. Allows time to get a drink or snack.)

- Allow for a 30-60 minute break. (This could be for lunch. Encourage people to go for a walk if weather permits.)

- Be sensitive to start and stop times if you are working across time zones.

- Open with an ice breaker like, "What countries have you visited?"

If you are interested in more tips and ideas for remote meetings, they are available in the *Creatives Lead Companion Workbook*. The ebook version can be found at creativeslead.com

Part 2
Working Out the Kinks

In this part, we are going to be focusing on you as a leader, adjusting your mindset, learning habits, and modeling healthy leadership values to propel you and your team successfully forward.

Week Four

Don't Be Afraid to Ask For Help

You may hit some rough patches as your team gets used to you and you get used to working with them. It's natural. It will smooth out—trust me. To minimize these rough spots, you will spend this week assessing and aligning your strengths and resource needs. You will also spend time in introspection, assessing the leader you are and want to become.

Week Five

Work it Out

Part of any endeavor includes conflict. We don't like it, but it happens. How you deal with issues when they arise can define you as a leader. This week you learn to deal with personal and team issues and how to mitigate conflict.

Week Six

Take Care of Yourself

You want to prove yourself as a valuable asset to the organization and team. It is easy to put in long hours and time on the weekends to stay on top of work, but don't neglect yourself! This week you'll learn that taking care of *you* is one of the best things you can do for your career, team, and those you love.

Creatives Lead

Don't Be Afraid to Ask for Help

You may hit some rough patches, as your team gets used to you and you get used to working with them. It's natural. It will smooth out—trust me. To minimize these rough spots, you will spend this week assessing and aligning your strengths, weaknesses and resource needs. You will also spend time in introspection, assessing the leader you are, and the leader you want to become.

- Set Up a Team That Is Strong Where You Are Weak
- Leadership Insecurity
- You Might Be a Micromanager If...
- How to Deal with Micromanagers
- Week 4 Practical Applications

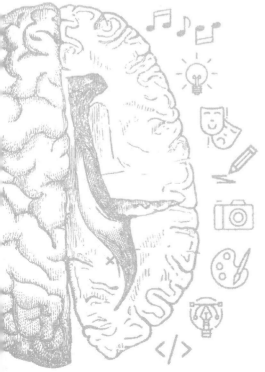

Creatives Lead

Chapter 11

Set Up a Team That Is Strong Where You Are Weak

No one likes to admit weaknesses.

Andrew was starting an organization from scratch. He recently left a company where he was not fond of the leadership style and company culture. He had ideas for a new organization that would be more modern in approach and not have the organizational baggage that many older companies acquire over the years.

With several committed friends, he held a meeting in his home to plan out the new organization. They knew they were only six strong at this point but mapped out the entire organization as to how they envisioned it growing over the subsequent five to six years.

"Okay, I am not good with finances," Andrew said. "Honestly, I am only good at writing, speaking, and getting people rallied behind a vision and goals."

"I handled finances at a previous job; I can take that on," Richard said.

"Okay, great! Now we have twenty-three more spots to fill," said Andrew, and that's the way the rest of the evening went. Each person candidly shared what they were good at doing and what they were not good at doing, but they were willing to take on multiple roles until they found the right person for each particular job.

Admitting Your Weaknesses

Does that sound like you, or do you feel that, as the new leader, you have to be able to do it all? Realistically, you realize at some level, you cannot do it all and guess what? Your team knows it. So why do some leaders act like they know it all and don't rely upon or seem to trust their teams?

"It's because I am the leader, and I am responsible!" you may be thinking. Well, you're right: You are responsible, but here are a few secrets. The best leaders know where they are weak and are not afraid to admit it—to themselves, their teams, and their leadership. The best leaders build a team that is strong where they are weak. They look to that team for support, advice, recommendations, and the skills and talent to do together what the leader could never do by himself.

"Fake It Till You Make It"

Have you ever heard that mantra in the modern business world? That is a stupid mantra because the only person you are fooling is yourself. Everyone else knows you're faking it. The longer you fake it, the less respect you will have.

What does a good leader do? A good leader knows his strengths and weaknesses, he will provide as much clarity as he can around an issue, he will ask good questions, he will trust and support the team, he will give praise when things go well, and he will take responsibility when things go wrong.

Know Your Strengths and Weaknesses

In week one, you should have taken the temperament assessment. This is a good place to begin to understand your unique wiring—what your strengths and weaknesses are and how to communicate them. Now, you will want to personally assess what you are good at skill-wise related to the team needs and goals. If there is a team member that has a strength where you are weak, don't let that bother you—lean into it, not away from it. When you're in a meeting with that individual, don't feel the need to comment or put your seal of approval on something you know very little about. Trust them—let them run with it. You need only ask questions to confirm direction, accountability, and due diligence on their part. Don't micromanage—lead where you are strong and be willing to let others lead where you are weak.

Provide Clarity

Let's face it: All leaders are uncertain at some level. You will not always have the answers or know what to do in a given situation. That is okay. It is better to be clear when you are uncertain than it is to pretend to have certainty on a topic. Don't be afraid and don't make stuff up. If you don't know something, admit it and let the team know you will find out—then get back to them with what you learn. You may only know the boundaries of a project, the budget, the absolute no's, or what to do next but not what the outcome will be, and that's okay. Regardless of what may happen, share what you do know and keep moving while you figure it out as a team.

Ask Good Questions

You don't have to be an expert on a topic or skill set, but you can always ask good questions. You are in a senior position because you have life experience that others on your team may not have yet acquired. You will also have information about projects based upon the peers you interact with and the other leaders you partner with in the organization. Ask open-ended questions of your team that spur them to think of:

- What is the end goal?
- Other creative possibilities and explorations
- Who does this impact?
- How will it increase sales/revenue/customer retention/etc.?
- When will this roll out?
- Why do we need it?

Unconvinced

?

One of the best questions a mentor shared with me was to ask a team member or larger group, "What do you think?" When a team seems stuck or they keep coming to you for solutions, put it back on them—ask, "What do you think we should do?" You'll be amazed how that simple little question can spur people into action and open the floodgates of possibilities.

Trust and Support the Team

Nothing gets a team more excited than to know that you trust and support them. Give them the opportunity to take ideas and run with them. You are there to keep them in between the guardrails so they don't crash and burn. When they know you have their backs, they are excited to come to work. Since you have learned their strengths, encourage them to grow and expand in these areas. Soon you'll find other leaders asking you how you created such a high-performing team.

Give Praise When Things Go Well

This seems like a no-brainer, but you'd be surprised how little praise is given in the workplace. Maybe you have experienced this yourself in a previous job. Maybe it's happening in your current job. If you do not receive praise, please don't withhold it from your team. What gets rewarded gets repeated! When others talk about *your* good work, place that squarely on the team's shoulders. If they are not with you when you receive a compliment, be sure to share it with them during your next team meeting. Too often, leaders receive praise and take it for themselves. It's easy to get an inflated ego as a result of this. Don't let that happen. Recognize you can't get the work done without the team and let them know that regularly.

Take Responsibility When Things Go Wrong

You may think this would be the hardest thing to do on the list, but it's really not, and your team will praise you for it. No one likes to fail. No one likes to be the bearer of bad news, but the reality is that mistakes happen, failure occurs, deadlines get missed, goals are not met, and the list goes on.

When that happens, what will you do? Will you blame it on the team? On someone else? On the timeline?

Be willing to take the hit for the team—take responsibility. If you have been communicating with your team, providing clarity and support, you should be able to minimize the issue. Why? Because you should have seen it coming already. Yet, at times there are things outside your control that can cause a project to go awry. Acknowledge it, learn from it, and put together a plan to move forward.

In Pat Lencioni's book, *The Four Obsessions of an Extraordinary Executive: A Leadership Fable,* setting up a team that is strong where you are weak is part of the first "obsession." Lencioni goes on to say:

> Members of cohesive teams know one another's strengths and weaknesses and don't hesitate to point them out. They also know something about one another's backgrounds, which helps them to understand why members think and act the way they do.[11]

Let's circle back to Andrew's story from the beginning of this chapter. Would you be surprised to learn his organization has grown and thrived over the last twenty-plus years? With a staff of several hundred people, the original team was able to hand off the areas in which they were weak and are now functioning in their areas of strength. The organization now impacts hundreds of thousands of people around the world, and it all started with this simple principle.

What are you waiting for?

Chapter 12
Leadership Insecurity

I talked with a friend yesterday who recently left a job. I was shocked and concerned to hear how the company and its culture had changed within a very short period of time. Over the course of five months, communication went from full disclosure to hidden agendas, from mission-minded to money-centered, from exciting to discouraging, and from encouraging to fearful and intimidating. What could bring on this hideous transformation in such a short time?

This is the result of leadership insecurity.

This leadership principle goes something like this: If things are dysfunctional at the top, it trickles down through the entire organization but, if things are healthy at the top, it too permeates the entire enterprise.

When a leader is insecure in their knowledge, capabilities, experience, relationship with peers, stockholders, the board of directors, or with other partners, disaster is headed their way. They are going to do whatever it takes to "prove" they are the boss and that they are in control—anything to bolster their self-esteem. Unknowingly, this spells death for the leader, their team and, quite possibly, the organization. Insecure leaders can kill enthusiasm, new ideas, and anything else that threatens them. You may feel "kill" is a harsh word, but this issue needs to be dealt with harshly, or it can spread like a malignant cancer. What do insecure leaders kill?

3 Things Insecure Leaders "Kill"

1. They kill community.
2. They kill culture.
3. They kill the company.

What's the Answer?

If you're the insecure leader–congratulations! At least you have recognized the fact that you are insecure or wrestle with insecurities. As such, you likely have a higher EQ (emotional intelligence) than most. The leader who is not in touch with himself will be doomed to wallow in self-pity, apathy, anger, and ego. Take some time to reflect on these questions and pinpoint your area(s) of insecurity.

- Can knowledge or experience be gained in order to combat the particular area you struggle with?
- Do you feel like you're trying to measure up to someone you are not?

Ideas: Take an educational course; read a book; dig in and get your hands dirty.

Don't try to be anyone else. Face the reality—you never will be able to meet your perceived standard. Be yourself, and if you do not like yourself, find out what you don't like and change it. Seek professional help if you need to. There is no shame in asking for help. Admitting a weakness is certainly better than continuing down a destructive path of pride.

What if I Report to an Insecure Leader?

If you report to an insecure leader, I am truly sorry for what you are going through. You need to evaluate the kind of working relationship you have with him. Think about these questions:

Can you confront them about their behavior?

If you're fortunate to have an open and honest relationship with your boss, let him know what you have observed or experienced. Let him know how it is impacting the department, division, or company. It does the leader no good if he blindly goes about business from day to day and has no feedback regarding the trail of bodies he is leaving behind.

Should you leave?

In some cases it may be that you have to get out of the unhealthy environment. "Save yourself," so to speak. This is by no means a simple decision and should not be a knee-jerk reaction either. Consider your options carefully, and if there is no way out other than to remove yourself, do so accordingly.

Other Scenarios

You manage the insecure leader:

If you recognize this harmful trait within your direct report, you need to be upfront and let him know it needs changing. Be proactive and brainstorm, or recommend solutions to get the leader back on a healthy track. It might be that the person is not cut out for leadership and should be removed. Be careful here and don't just fire the individual. Once again, be upfront and let them know the severity of the situation. Work through it together for their good and yours.

You're about to hire a leader:

Do your homework. Just because the candidate is a nice person and has a good sense of humor does not make him a leader. As the saying goes: "Measure twice and cut once" (see chapter 3: When Hiring). Remember when interviewing the candidate, get him to talk and tell stories of how he handled tough situations. Past behavior is often a predictor of future behavior. Do not let the urgent need to fill a position dictate hiring the *first good person* for the job. Better to pass by a *good* candidate in order to find the *best* candidate.

Final Thoughts

Insecurity has been described as a war in an unhealthy mind. We all want healthy, thriving companies—who doesn't? Those who lead must have a healthy, balanced attitude and outlook. Take time to be introspective. Play to your strengths and be secure in who you are.

Chapter 13

You Might Be a Micromanager If…

Aron loved his job in the marketing department. He had been hired four years earlier as a junior designer and was now a senior designer, working on some innovative and growing projects. He enjoyed taking on new projects and stretching his skills. He had recently been asked to learn a digital animation package and help fill in since the previous animator had resigned from the company. Aron was a team player and was happy to help, even though his current workload would not diminish. He felt like he was finally in his sweet spot and relished the new challenges.

In the previous few weeks, Aron's hiring manager had moved to another company. Jamie, his new manager, who had been over the communications department, was now in charge of both the marketing and communications departments. Aron quickly learned that Jamie had little experience in the work and projects Aron was involved in. Jamie frequently came by his desk to ask him what he was doing. This wasn't so bad, except it became clear to Aron that Jamie was not interested in the projects as much as he was interested in knowing Aron was busy working.

Throughout the year, Aron met all his deadlines in spite of the added work and new status reports that Jamie kept insisting on. When it came time for his annual review, Aron was totally demoralized. Instead of recognizing his extra efforts while staying on top of his workload, Jamie hammered on one small project that popped up the previous month. A project had come to Aron's desk as a "rush job" for a new album cover design. Aron worked hard to meet the initial deadline but was not able to complete all the change requests until several days later. That one missed deadline ended up being the summary statement for Aron's entire year of work. The next day, Aron gathered some boxes from the shipping department. "Unless something changes here, I am prepared to pack up and leave," he said to himself. "Nothing is worth this kind of abuse."

Fortunately, within six months, Jamie left the company to pursue another job. Aron felt like a weight had been lifted off his shoulders, but the emotional damage had been done. What was his next leader going to be like?

In our last chapter we discussed the impact of insecure leadership. Sometimes insecurities can cause us to micromanage. Everyone dislikes a micromanager. Maybe your EQ is low, and you're not sure what this kind of behavior looks like. Like Aron, what if you work with a micromanager? Or worse, what if you are one? Here are some tell-tale signs. Take a look and see how many apply to you or those around you.

- Only *you* can do the job.
- You're always looking over your employees' shoulders.
- You are spending $10.00 to save $1.00.
- You want to be CC'd on every email sent by team members.
- There's only one way to get things done–your way.
- You're intimidated by those around you.
- You come in early and stay late most all the time. (You also might be a workaholic.)
- You time your staff coming in the door but not when they're leaving.
- You change your mind often and almost always reverse your decision.
- You're so consumed with the details, you lose sight of the big picture.
- You like to have submissive subordinates.

- You hate to respond to emails or put anything in writing.
- You are anxious most of the time and feel your incompetence will be revealed.
- You do not like to see your people develop professionally nor as a person.
- You're good at humiliating people and making them feel marginalized.
- You do not relinquish your authority.
- You quickly punish others' mistakes but hide your own.
- You overload yourself and those around you.
- You do not trust others.
- You lie often.
- You often blame others.
- You break promises easily—especially when keeping them is inconvenient.
- Being vulnerable frightens you.
- You like to surround yourself with "yes men," brown-nosers, and boot-lickers.
- You nitpick during performance reviews.
- You have to approve every little thing.
- You isolate your staff from contact outside your area of authority.
- You distort information.
- You fear accountability.
- You personalize disagreements.
- You take offense at this list.

If many of these ring true for you, get some professional help quickly! Many counselors and psychiatrists acknowledge that this behavior is psychopathic and in need of help. Your spouse, family, staff, company, vendors, partners, and board will be glad you did.

If you work with a micromanager, the next chapter will show you how to deal with them in a healthy way that won't stress you out or leave you running and screaming from your office. Move on when you're ready.

Chapter 14
How to Deal With Toxic Relationships

Working hard was nothing new to Vihaan. He was in a service and support role, already juggling efforts in a matrix-managed organization. He supported his boss and two other leaders, including Max, a new leader.

Little did Vihaan expect the kind of working environment he was about to encounter. Even though he had worked with Max in the past, he had never experienced this level of extreme toxic behavior. The anger and vehemence with a dash of micromanagement had him questioning Max's sanity.

While in one discussion with Max, they had a disagreement about an operational aspect. Vihaan suggested one way, and Max pushed back aggressively.

"Take a moment to think," Max said.

"Think about what?"

"I have the ear of the CEO," Max threatened.

After the shock of this encounter, Vihaan reflected on the conversation with Max. "I have survived worse," he thought. "Max can't abuse me! I have been through junior college and college in India. That was an extremely rigid system—a very perfectionistic environment. I have pushed through hard and often unrealistic expectations as a student. Try creating sixteen drawings, each taking sixteen hours, and then having them ripped up in front of your face? Four years of engineering school was insane! I found ways to survive. I went through hell. I learned in college how to deal with any situation for life! What's the worst you can do to me? Fire me? I am not gonna let you threaten me!"

Several days later, Max came into his office and began yelling and banging on the table.

"Why didn't you do what I asked you to?!" he screamed.

"Because my boss told me not to. You need to take it up with him," Vihaan said.

After this unmerited temper tantrum, Max stormed out slamming the door behind him.

A week later, Vihaan became aware of an upcoming meeting. He asked Max about the meeting in order to prepare. As they walked into a stairwell, Max went off on Vihaan.

"Who do you think you are? I don't need to tell you who I am meeting with!"

Vihaan was taken aback, this time feeling threatened. Once again, Max stormed off.

Unfortunately, after being exposed to this toxic behavior over a period of time, Vihaan found himself not caring about work at all. He came in, did his job, and left every day. No enthusiasm. No passion for what he was doing. It was as if the life had been sucked out of Vihaan. He briefly thought about reporting Max to HR but had gotten to the point where he did not care.

"Why bother?" Vihaan thought, "He's not gonna change."

Do any of these qualities sound familiar to you? Are they qualities in you or ones you have experienced in others?

We are going to assume you are not a jerk, but you work with or for one. Don't be dismayed. Here are strategies for dealing with this kind of controlling individual.

In his book, *My Way or the Highway: The Micromanagement Survival Guide*,[12] Harry Chambers describes the destructive behavior patterns of this kind of manager. Below are listed several strategies you can use to effectively deal with and survive the rigors of working for a micromanager:

Find out his agenda and goals - Determine what's really important to him, then work with him—not against him.

Take initiative with information - Don't wait to be asked for information. Find out what the micromanager needs to feel confident and comfortable, then get it to him—ahead of time.

Practice regular communication - No one fears inertia more than the micromanager. Show that you're working on priority projects by communicating in three specific terms— awareness, reassurance, and timelines.

Be clear on expectations - Clarify your agreements in a trail of memos and emails.

Renegotiate priorities - Come up with a simple, straightforward method—such as a numerical or a color-coded system—for renegotiating the ever-shifting priorities.

Be preemptive on deadlines - The micromanager loves to impose and even distort deadlines. Be the first to talk—offering a timeline for when you can do a task (not when you can't).

Play by the rules - The micromanager enjoys catching people in the act. Avoid being an easy target and play by the rules— particularly on policies regarding time and technology.

Learn from others - The micromanager backs off with some people more than others. Watch those individuals closely to learn the secrets of their success.

Pick your battles - The micromanager will go to war on every issue. Don't try to match him. Instead, choose the battles that are most important to you.

Now let's discuss the more volatile relationships like Vihaan and Max's above. What can you do when the person is a narcissistic, aggressive, gossiping glory-seeker who intimidates by bullying?

Training

Try to detect toxic issues as soon as possible. This allows you to offer, someone like Max, training or education if needed.[13]

Set Guardrails

Setting parameters around the relationship is usually necessary. Try not to meet alone or within a space where anything said becomes your word against his.

Watch Yourself

We are all capable of exhibiting toxic behavior. Learn to look for it in yourself as well as others. Don't stand for it and make sure others don't as well.

Reporting System

Make sure there is a system in place to report toxic behaviors without retaliation. This can be an anonymous reporting system or some other procedure that protects people.[14]

Last Resort

As a leader, termination may be the only option for an offending employee. "Be sure your employee manual includes these behaviors as unacceptable and that they can be used as grounds for termination. Document all incidents and any talks or other forms of communication with the employee prior to any termination or suspension for their behaviors."[15]

As a new leader, you're recognizing that managing people can be tough. Dealing with micromanagers and toxic relationships should never be commonplace. If you've experienced working for that kind of individual, I am truly sorry. Moving forward, you can use the tactics listed here. Yet, remember how it felt when you were in that situation. Don't be that kind of leader. Don't put your people through that emotional nightmare. Learn from it and don't be afraid to ask for help.

Applications for Week 4

While your team is forming, it will likely be going through a "storming" phase as people get used to you, other new hires, or as you get used to them. Understanding the strengths and weaknesses of you and your team can help propel you toward success.

Practical Applications

This week you will do three things:

1. Create Team Profile Sheets (TPS).
2. Spend time doing a Personal Leadership Evaluation (PLE).
3. Conduct your team off-site.

Why create a TPS? To start a human resource file for each member and to assess the team as a whole; do they communicate well? Do they collaborate well? Do they have the resources/training they need to get their jobs done? Are people aligned to projects based on their strengths? Are they aligned to each other properly? (Strength/weakness, mentoring, etc.)

The TPS could be something you have the team do during the off-site. Pass around blank templates and ask each team member to fill out their own. You can gather them up afterward and keep them handy for one-on-one meetings or when discussing career development. The TPS Template is also available in the *Creatives Lead Companion Workbook©*.

TPS Template

Team Member Name:	Team Member Picture
Start Date:	
Key Contacts:	

Personal mission:	Personal passion:
Strengths:	Weaknesses:
Notes:	
Goals:	
Communication Style:	
Highlights:	
Projects:	

Personal Leadership Evaluation

What kind of leader do you want to be?

Grab a notebook, your personal journal, or Notes app on your electronic device and set aside thirty or forty-five minutes to think about and capture the following:

1. What are the qualities you have admired in your current or previous leaders?
2. What are the qualities in leaders that have frustrated you?
3. List what you are personally passionate about.
4. List what frustrates you personally.
5. Who can you ask to mentor you? (This can be related to work or other areas of life you feel you can improve upon.)

6. Create an action plan based on what you've captured.

- How will you become the leader you want to be?

- How do you need to change and grow?

- How and when will you get the help you need?

Conduct Your Team Off-site

If not this week, then next week at the latest, you should be hosting your team's off-site meeting. Remember to use the resources provided in Week 3 Practical Applications. You should have plenty to discuss. Afterward, drop me a note at creativeslead.com to tell me how it went.

Creatives Lead

Work It Out

Part of any endeavor includes conflict. We don't like it, but it happens. How you deal with issues when they arise can define you as a leader. This week you will learn how to be a leader worth following, how to deal with personal and team issues, and how to mitigate conflict.

- The 10 Commandments for Leadership
- Show Restraint
- Work Through Issues
- Week 5 Practical Applications

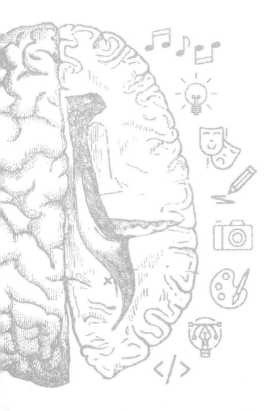

Creatives Lead

Chapter 15
The 10 Commandments for Leadership

Heron had been working in his organization for almost ten years as an individual contributor. He liked the work. It was regular and predictable. However, now he had children, and a little more money would be nice to help cover growing expenses. A new senior position came open. Heron discussed the opening with his leadership and decided to apply. As it turned out, he got the new role. He was both excited and intimidated.

For three months he struggled with his new responsibilities. He was quickly realizing that he would rather be back in his old position because he knew what to do—it was second nature for him. He had done it for years, and it was comfortable.

He surprised everyone when he asked to be moved back into his old job. For Heron, he learned that the politics of leadership were too stressful for him. He could not make the transition mentally or emotionally to be the leader that the team needed. He felt at ease and safe where he had been, not having to deal with the personnel issues that often came with leadership roles. Just as surprising, his leadership recognized Heron was floundering and not thriving. They recognized his value and contribution to the organization and worked it out so he could move back into his previous position.

So, what am I saying here? I am not saying you should abandon your new leadership role because it feels uncomfortable or hard. What I am saying is *know* yourself. Can you thrive in tough interpersonal relationships? Can you find a way where there doesn't seem to be a way? Can you be calm and set a good example for your team in the face of adversity?

Leaders don't always start out as leaders unless, like me, you start your own company. More often, we started out as production artists or junior designers, then move up to full-fledged designers, then someone puts us in a leadership position whether out of necessity or because we have applied for the senior role. Yet, as a new leader, the inclination is to drift back to what we know and have done in the past (i.e. designing). It is a safe space for us. Dealing with people and personalities can be taxing, and sometimes you just want to go back to "normal." What often gets missed here is the connection we should make with those whom we lead and those outside our team whom we work with.

Everyone is looking for someone to follow—to take a cue from. Set an example that others will want to follow. I got this list below from Don Boykin (originally titled, *What I Wish I Had Known Before I Got into Management*). I hope you find it as helpful as I did when I was a new leader.

The 10 Commandments

1. It is always about people and relationships.

We tend to focus on the work rather than the people. Don't do it! We have to keep our eyes on the people.

2. It's more about being than doing.

Dr. Henry Blackaby says that leadership development is synonymous with personal growth. The best thing a leader can do for his organization is to grow personally.

You can't lead by trying to be someone else. It's faulty to try to lead by imitating someone else. Their methods may work, but you cannot *be* them. Make the style your own.

3. You lead by serving.

Check your motivation—don't use people—use tools, but never use or abuse people. Become a servant leader (more on this in Part 3).

4. Your employees are your most important resource.

Tied to number three—a leader who serves—if you don't understand this, you have failed as a leader.

5. Be the first one in and the last one out.

Not really in reference to hours; in relation to your involvement. Remember, you're setting the example for others to follow.

6. You need to achieve critical business objectives while satisfying people's personal needs.

This comes from getting to know your people. Know their strengths and weaknesses. Know their ambitions and goals. This allows you to uniquely position your people per objective to get the job done while inspiring morale.

7. Feedback is important to leadership.

Be honest with your people. Tell them what they need to know—point out strengths as well as weaknesses. Be careful not to neglect your most skilled people and do not take them for granted.

During performance reviews, be specific. Don't just tell them what needs work—tell them what they can do to get where you'd like to see them.

8. Performance achievement is a shared responsibility.

It is not enough to simply expect the people to get there. You, as the leaders, have to help them to do it.

9. You are a coach and a catalyst.

Coaches celebrate, encourage, suffer, teach, rise, and fall along with the team while a catalyst is someone who sparks actions in others.

10. Open communication results from sharing your thoughts, reasoning, and feelings.

When you listen and understand, you leave yourself open and approachable. You gain trust. Be vulnerable. Show them your thoughts and feelings. Help them understand your perspective and feelings. This is hard for many—especially if you're insecure. Provide support without removing responsibility. Don't just move them over and do it yourself. Help them to succeed on their own!

Golden Rule

A gifted and competent leader will display genuine humility. Don't give them your ego and arrogance. If you are serving them, there isn't room for your pride. Work out your personal and team issues early.

There is a lot packed into those commandments. They can take years to master, but some leaders have never learned them and have no desire to. I hope that is not you. Like Heron, you might feel intimidated, fearful, and out of your element. Be willing to learn. You're likely reading this book because you want to learn. It is in the tough times that we often learn the most—the most about ourselves and others.

Now, if only others shared your mindset. Right? We all learn at differing rates and in different ways. Don't let relational issues discourage you. Learn to show restraint and self-control. We will discuss this topic in the next chapter.

Chapter 16

Show Restraint

restraint

noun

restraint: self-control, self-restraint, self-discipline, control, moderation, prudence, judiciousness, abstemiousness.

This definition became real to me when my creative director walked into my office one day. It was obvious she was flustered and upset.

"Hey Jae, what's up?" I asked.

Jae walked over to my desk. I could see she was biting her lip—a sign she was stressed.

"I don't know what's going on with Johan. I have asked him several times to change a design, and every time I review his work, nothing has changed, and he has gone in the opposite direction of what I asked!" she said.

I had noticed the same thing about Johan during a review when I had given him some feedback. It was like he was not listening and went off and did his own thing.

"I hear you," I said. "I have noticed the same thing."

I found myself starting to get upset with Johan. If he was not taking direction from me or the creative director, then I needed to straighten him out quickly. Deadlines were approaching, and we did not have time to run in circles or in another direction.

"Tell you what," I said. "I am going to meet with him and get this straightened out."

I was ready to power up. I was ready to exert my positional power and tell Johan to get his act together or else find a warning in his personnel file. He had had opportunities to listen and change several times, but this was obviously becoming a problem.

Thank goodness I did not meet with Johan that same day. I had a mentor who had shared with me to take a step back anytime I found myself getting emotional about an issue. And so I did. I spent a good part of the evening in introspection and tried to put myself in Johan's shoes.

"Maybe there was more to this than what we were seeing," I thought.

The next day, Johan met me in my office. He was looking a little sheepish as he sat down.

"What's going on, Johan?"

That was all I said.

I could have said, "What's wrong with you? Do you have a problem taking direction? Why are you not doing what we've asked? Do I need to step in and do your job?"

But I didn't.

That simple open-ended question delivered in a non-judgmental way opened the door to a more productive conversation. Johan talked about the stress he was under at home and how it was impacting his concentration at work. He expressed how bad he felt about the job he was doing but didn't know what to do about it. I then took the time to assure him that he was a valuable member of the team and that we needed him to be honest and up front if he was unable to deliver what was expected of him. I had other employees with lower workloads that could pitch in and help him out. He thanked me for caring and understanding and promised to let me and Jae know when he needed assistance.

Watch What You Say and Hear

You're now the boss. You hold positional power. People watch what you say and do.

They really do.

Such bad writing

As the boss, it can be easy to tell people what to do and abuse your power. Many succumb to the power of being in charge. You should not.

One of the hardest things about being the leader is that you are under scrutiny. You are accountable for the work your team/department/division does. You have goals, Key Performance Indicators (KPI's), and Objective and Key Results (OKR's) that you will be measured against. You have been put in this position because you're expected to get the job done. This can produce a huge amount of pressure and stress. But as a new leader, you cannot let it show because your people are watching everything you say and do.

Jeffrey Fox, founder of Fox&Co. said, "A [leader's] whisper is like a lion's roar."[16] As a leader, a random thought or idea voiced can be perceived as an order or work request. I have witnessed firsthand how a leader can be verbally ideating, spit-balling, or processing solutions, and the people around her take it as mandatory needs and requirements. Think about what you say, to whom, and how you say it. Your whisper is like a roar.

New employees in the workforce

New employees are energetic and eager to please and show their merit. As the boss, what you say to them and how you say it are critical and formative as they are new to the workforce. Balance praise with careful critique. Encourage critical thinking and problem solving (See chapter 11.) Also, be careful not to become too casual with them, but let them know you sincerely care about their welfare and career. Remember, words have power to give life or cause despair. New employees will often hang on your every word.

Yes-men (or women/person)

Be careful not to surround yourself with people who say what you want to hear. There are those in the workplace who seek admiration and advancement through sycophantic behavior. You know them. You have seen them in action. Don't be one, and don't surround yourself with them. Your other employees are not fooled. They will watch how you respond in situations. Consequently, they will either admire you or loathe you.

Say no to yes-men.

Watch What You Do

Finally, your actions have implications. The phrase, "Actions speak louder than words" is true. Do you have to be first? Do you need to have the close parking space or swanky office view? Do you build people up or beat them down? Do you talk more than listen?

What is your reputation?

How you behave distinguishes you as either a manager that people want to work with or one that people want to avoid. To coin a phrase from Roz of Pixar's Monsters Inc.® your employees are watching—always watching.

Had I come into the conversation with Johan ready to steamroll him, we never would have gotten to this point of understanding and collaboration. Johan would have been on the defensive and shut down. All I would have done was add to his stress.

Are you able to restrain yourself in matters like Jae and Johan? Can you demonstrate self-control and personal discipline when it comes to leadership? Much hangs in the balance. Your reputation and your career go hand in hand. Both what you say and what you do form your reputation. Showing restraint is a sign of leadership maturity and responsibility.

When you are tempted to power-up and use your position, pause for a moment. Be willing to work out any misperceptions and misunderstandings. Show restraint, be real, and your people will reward you with their admiration and engagement.

Chapter 17
Work Through the Issues

Bryan called me into his office.

I wasn't sure what to expect, but I had an idea when I saw Gladice sitting across from Bryan's desk. Both Gladice and I had recently been promoted. In our careers as user experience designers, we had both come from similar backgrounds and done the same kinds of work. In our new roles, Gladice was aligned more to visuals and overseeing the designers. I was aligned more to strategy and overseeing the experience architects. The practices within each discipline overlap some, and that area of overlap had been causing issues with Gladice and the designers.

The designers felt the architects were doing part of their job, and it was frustrating them. The architecture renderings were in a higher fidelity than typical documents. Some designers were wondering if they were hired to design or just execute what the architects had laid out.

In my mind, this could have been circumvented if the designers had been candid and had a conversation with their teammates. Yet, as you learned in week one of this book, everyone has differing temperaments, and creatives in general are not good at confrontation.

Bryan shared the reason for our meeting, confirming my suspicions. He then asked us to talk through the issues.

"I am sorry, Gladice, that this has been a point of frustration for the designers," I began. "How can we work together to make this better for everyone?" That diffused the tension in the room. We were then able to discuss openly the friction in the team and solutions for how they could work better together.

"Guys, I am really impressed with how you handled yourselves and this situation," Bryan said afterward. "I am really proud of you both."

I was glad as well that Bryan had created an environment of trust. An environment where the team could have candid conversations and work through issues and disagreements.

In the past, I have jokingly told friends that the problem with work is that it involves *people*. While it is a joke, many jokes contain a little bit of reality that we can often relate to and find somewhat humorous as a result. The reality is: working with people can be hard and challenging. As a leader, you have to be willing to work through all the issues and difficulties that may arise. It's not easy because our nature is to recoil from things that make us feel pain or are uncomfortable.

Personnel Disagreements

Often in creative teams, not only are there differing personalities and work styles, but there can be differing interpretations to problems the team is trying to solve. These differences can be a toxic combination if not handled well. You know this. You've experienced it, I'm sure.

"The problem we are trying to solve is A," says one employee.

"No, the problem we are trying to solve is B," says another.

"You are both wrong, it's A *and* B," says a third.

Who is right? All sides are passionate about what they are trying to solve. They all want the best solution and to do the best creative work.

Create settings to work through disagreements in real time.

Most often these take the form of regular critiques. One challenge here is many creatives see their work as an expression of themselves. When their work is critiqued, they can feel it as personal criticism. It is not. Be sure to set this expectation early and often.

Make sure everyone is heard.

During critiques you need to make sure there is only one conversation going on at a time. Don't let people talk over each other. Don't let side conversations happen. Show respect to the person who is presenting. Sometimes you will have to call on a quiet team member to get her to engage. This should be a trusting environment, where the best ideas, thoughts, and feedback bubble to the top.

No response implies agreement.

Let the team know that you need their thoughts and ideas. To make sure these get voiced, set the expectation that everyone needs to speak up during meetings and critiques. If you have built a trusting team, there should be no excuse for not participating. If team members feel it is not safe to share or they need time to process their thoughts, give them a deadline for feedback. The goal is to insure everyone has been heard. You do not want anyone on the team gossiping or complaining after the meeting.

Gossip Grapevine

Let me just say up front, I hate the gossip grapevine. I know "hate" is a strong word. I simply detest gossip. It does no good whatsoever. It only causes tension, fear, and derision.

The best way I found to stop this is to be open and honest with your people. Build trust with them. Let them know you are available for all their questions.

ALL questions.

Also, let them know that there will be some things you cannot answer, but there is nothing to hide. Important leadership and company communication often need to be synchronized, and that takes time. Some messages need preparation to roll out.

Creative people are notorious for being curious. As such, they can often make assumptions about a variety of work-related issues. Let people know gossip will not be tolerated, and that it does no good. If anyone starts to gossip, their co-workers should encourage them to come to you directly for answers.

Unproductivity

When there are issues with the team and there is gossip, there can also be lack of productivity. This can lead to churn on a daily basis. The team stalls and doesn't get work done.

On the other hand, when there is communication and trust, there will more likely be engagement. As a new leader, you are setting the example. Being open and transparent will go a long way toward creating employee engagement.

When you see unproductivity in your team, you need to deal with it quickly. Address any issues head on. Gather the team together and find out what's going on. If necessary, meet with team members one on one to assess the situation. In the end, you need to act on any solutions and be sure to follow up. Let your team know what and how you're addressing the issues.

People can be challenging to work with. You experienced it before you got into management, and now you're being looked to as the leader. You are expected to set the tone and create the environment to work through team issues. The best way you can do that is by creating an atmosphere of trust and openness. Work through disagreements and conflicts in real time, make sure everyone is heard, and do not stand for gossip or backbiting.

Applications for Week 5

Keeping your finger on the pulse of any issues (personal or team related), and creating an environment for discussing them are the keys to this week's applications.

Practical Applications

You will do two things this week:

1. Begin using a journal.
2. Begin holding team retrospectives.

Begin Using a Journal

I have rotated between a composition notebook, sketchbook, and various planners throughout the years. I use them for tracking to-do's, note-taking, sketching, ideation and more. Get what suits you best. You will use this for a variety of things, but for this week, it will act as a personal journal. (The *Creatives Lead Companion Workbook©* also includes these pages.)

As you meet with your staff and work through team performance issues, be sensitive to your thoughts and emotions. Do you find yourself getting easily angered? Do you find yourself getting easily frustrated or stressed? Do you find yourself withdrawing or abdicating your responsibility as a leader? Monitor yourself through the week.

Create three columns and label each: Situation, Initial Thoughts, and Final Action. Use the rows for each day of the week, and add to them at the start of each new day.

past issues for me

SITUATION	INITIAL THOUGHTS	FINAL ACTION	RESULTS
MONDAY - Johan not following creative direction; causing frustration across the team; collaboration issues?	Found myself getting upset and mad that we are wasting time; maybe putting a warning in his HR file will motivate him	Don't know all the details so I am going to meet with him and just ask "What's going on?" and see how he responds; I want to keep him as an employee and keep him engaged	The conversation went well. We discussed his performance and agreed on a regular check-in for accountability.
TUESDAY - Syrina trying to do too much and crossing into the work that others are responsible for; Causing confusion with the team. ———————— Dhavee is quiet and not communicating with the team; not sure what he is doing	I think some coaching and mentoring might be needed. Her last company used her as a "team of one" but that is not the case here. ———————— What has he been up to? He comes in late and leaves early - not good. Other team members see this too and could cause issues.	I will set up a 1x1 to share my observations. Let her know I appreciate her hard work. I have also set up a senior person to mentor her and be an object source. ———————— Need to set up 1x1 and ask him what's going on? Let him know I care about him and the work he is doing. Feel lack of communication leads to lack of awareness of project work and status...	
WEDNESDAY			

THURSDAY			
FRIDAY			

You will record each day's situations that need handling and your initial thoughts. That's all you will record each day. At the beginning of the next day and each subsequent workday, you will start the morning reviewing the previous day's situation and plan your related action. Giving yourself a minimum of twenty-four hours should be helpful in letting any initial emotional outbursts subside. You should be able to think more clearly about your final actions. Do this for the entire week.

Set Up and Conduct a Regular Team Retrospective

If you have been in the digital space, you may be familiar with Agile methodologies. One of the team practices is a retrospective or "retro." For your purposes, you want to create an environment where the team can build trust and share as you all work out the kinks and begin to normalize. The cadence of the retro is up to you and the team to decide—it could be once a week, once every other week, or at a minimum, once a month.

A typical retro is broken into the following parts:

1. Setting the Stage

2. What Went Well?

3. What Needs Improvement?

4. Next Steps (or Actions)

Preparation

If you are together, use a whiteboard or wall with individual Post-It® stickies. If you use stickie notes, use a common color for each phase of discussion (i.e. What went well = green, Needs improvement = red, etc.). If you are remote and have access to a collaborative tool like Mural® or InVision® Freehand, then set up a space for each discussion phase and let the team members add to each space in turn. If you don't have a digital collaboration tool, one person can screen-share something like a PowerPoint document, ask all other teammates to paste their notes into your chat (i.e. Skype, WebEx, etc.) while the one sharing copies the information to the shared document for all to see.

Setting the Stage

Make sure the team knows the time frame being discussed. If you don't have a facilitator, ask for a volunteer or choose one. You can also have a different team member facilitate each part of the discussion for a fresh perspective.

Remind the team not to make this time personal or take it personally. They should listen and respond with an open mind remembering that every experience is valid. Set a time frame for discussing each topic. You can even set a timer to help focus the team. Finally, encourage the team not to play the blame game but to have a mindset of continuous improvement.

What Went Well?

You will use an appropriate method to capture the team feedback. You want everyone to take part and to see what others are adding. Set your timer and begin. Have each team member capture individual thoughts/ideas of what went well over the agreed period of time. When time runs out, move to the next part.

What Needs Improvement?

Just like the one above, set your timer and have each team member capture notes/thoughts/ideas about what needs improvement. Remember, this is about actions and outcomes and not to be directed at any specific person. Once again, when the timer runs out, move to the next part.

Take a moment here before moving on to review the two parts you have just completed. Have each person share their thoughts and clarify any misunderstandings. You can even group the thoughts and ideas where it makes sense.

Next Steps

Now it's time to discuss specific steps and action items the team can take to improve or remove roadblocks. Have everyone brainstorm these and put one thought or idea per stickie or line. You can even assign these to particular team members afterward. Be sure to follow up a week later to see how much progress is being made. Are you getting to the root of your problems?

A final word about timing. I have found that thirty minutes to one hour is about right for a retro. You can break it up like this:

- Setting the Stage - five minutes
- What Went Well - ten minutes
- What Needs Improvement - ten minutes
- Review with Group - fifteen minutes
- Next Steps and Assignments - twenty minutes

Retros are meant be customized, so feel free to make them your own. Experiment and work with your team until this becomes second nature.

Have fun!

Week 6
Take Care of Yourself

You want to prove yourself as a valuable asset to the organization and team. It is easy to put in long hours and time on the weekends to stay on top of work, but don't neglect yourself! This week you'll learn that taking care of you is one of the best things you can do for your career, team, and those you love.

- The Value of Triangles
- Go Out and Play
- Mandatory Ping-Pong
- Week 6 Practical Applications

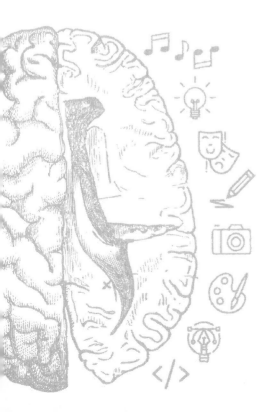

Chapter 18
The Value of Triangles

Dave was a wizard with a racket.

"Ten serving two."

"Pah-kow!" the racquetball sounded as Dave served. He always served to my backhand.

"Squeek!" The ball died in the back corner as I slammed into the wall trying desperately to return his serve.

"Eleven serving two…" he said with a smirk.

"Oh, shut up and serve the ball."

This time he tried it low and fast to my forehand side, and I was able to get the edge of my racket on the ball—sending it in a lazy arc to the front wall.

Dave was on it in a second and offered a light touch, causing me to run like a wheezing madman to the front before the ball would bounce twice on the floor.

I made it!

With my body between him and the ball, I gave it a shot off the front angling toward the back corner. Ha! I knew who would be sprinting now.

Unfortunately, instead of the ball dying in the corner as I intended, it bounced off the back wall parallel to the side wall. Dave had enough room to get his racket on it and sent the ball speeding toward the ceiling.

While I was backing up, the ball came off the ceiling, hitting the front wall at such an angle and velocity that it bounced off the floor and over my head. I jumped trying to get a piece of the little blue ball. I knew that if I missed, it would hit the floor again behind me and the point would be Dave's.

I missed.

"Woohoo!" he shouted as he took his customary victory lap around the court. "Every day is Kreesmahs!" he said in his thick Nigerian accent.

Dave went on to win that game—like he did every racquetball game we played. I tried playing tennis with him. He beat me. I even tried playing Badminton with him. Did you know a birdie could actually sting?

Dave majored in exercise physiology. He loved to exercise and play sports. His job was a trainer, and he was very good at it. Spending time with Dave taught me the need to take care of myself physically, mentally, and emotionally.

Growing up, I had always been active. I played basketball, a year of baseball (not my go-to sport), tennis, and racquetball throughout college (mostly with Dave). I also golfed, ran a half-dozen road races, studied martial arts for many years, and played drums. Yes, drumming can be quite strenuous if you're aggressively playing a full drum set over the course of several hours. I also tried roller hockey for a while.

As I got older and started a family, I took notice of several points:

- Golf got expensive, and I needed to use my income for other things.
- I started getting tendonitis in one of my knees, so running had to stop.
- I didn't heal from the sparring and bruising as quickly as I used to, so martial arts slowed down considerably.
- My lower back got sore from drumming long hours plus our new home had no place to set up my kit, so that stopped.
- My wife and I had children, and I wanted to spend more time with them.

At each of these points I had to assess the season of life I was in as well as the quality of life I wanted to have as I got older. Many of these activities had to take a back seat to other life priorities.

You may be, or soon will be, experiencing these same decision points in your life. I hope you will always keep in mind what my friend and other mentors have told me throughout the years—taking care of yourself physically, mentally, and emotionally is an essential part of being a leader.

All Good Things Come in Three's

An equilateral triangle has three equal sides. Each of the practices stated above are a point on the triangle as they each have the same value. No one is greater than the other. Doing one or two do not have the same value as doing all three. And doing one or two better than another does not have the same value as doing the best you can in each practice. All three need equal care and priority.

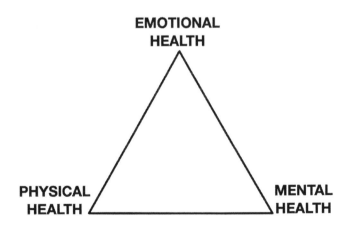

I am not going to belabor these points here because there are plenty of other books, websites, and articles that explore these topics in greater detail. However, I do want to stress the value these three practices will bring to you, your team, and your family.

Value of Physical Health

Regular Exercise

Higher energy levels - Increases energy, even for those with chronic illness.

Better sleep - Helps you relax and stimulates recuperation during sleep.

Can help with weight loss - Increases your metabolism, burning more calories.[17]

Muscle tone and bone strength - Helps build muscle and bone strength.

Pain reduction - Reduces chronic pain and enhances pain tolerance.

Brain health and mental acuity - Can improve mood and reduce stress/anxiety.

Natural Nutrition

Consistent energy levels - Increases stamina throughout the day without the crash-n-burn.

Healthy weight - Influences your weight and health by eating natural vs. processed foods.

Boosted immune system - Reduces risk for hypertension, diabetes, and heart disease.

Improved skin condition - Helps protect your skin against the sun's damaging effects.[18]

A note about water: it is a valuable part of physical health. Drinking water is part of good nutrition. Drinking enough water (preferably filtered) helps with hunger, headaches, and energy levels throughout the day.

Value of Mental Health

Self-confidence - Helps you face new situations or new people you interact with.

Optimism - Helps you approach plans and situations with a positive outlook.

Goal setting - Motivates beyond just the present and anticipates the
  future.
Self esteem - Provides confidence in your abilities and self-respect.[19]
A note about sleep:[20] it is a valuable part of mental health. While the
deepest sleep is best physiologically for getting rest and boosting your
immune system, REM (rapid eye movement) sleep enhances learning,
memory, and is great for mental health.

Value of Emotional Health

Better self-talk - Helps you feel positive when dealing with life's
  challenges.
Quality relationships - Enhances your mood, making you more
  pleasant socially.
Less stress - Reduces feelings of sadness and depression.[21]
Contentment - Helps you learn to be at ease in any situation.
A note about spiritual health (in case you've been wondering): An
article by Dr. David H. Olson, professor of family social science at the
University of Minnesota, discusses the premarital/marriage assessment
tool, *Prepare/Enrich*.[22] From its beginnings in 1978, the assessment
"continues to adapt and react to the changing reality of relationships
through continued research."[23] Of interest is a section on spiritual beliefs.
Regardless of where you stand—with or without a belief system, the
research showed that having similar spiritual beliefs with those you're
closest to helps mitigate relational problems, promotes healthier premarital
and marital relationships, and results in a better life.

I remember going through art school. Often my daily diet consisted of
fast food for breakfast, crackers and a soda for lunch, and pizza or fried
chicken for dinner. They were fast and easy-access foods. At the time, I was
more interested in my creative pursuits than long-term physical, mental, or
emotional pursuits. As I have gotten older, I have had the benefit of
watching, listening to, and meeting with leaders I admire. All of them adhere
to these three practices. There is value in triangles. It is not too late. You can

begin these practices too! If you're already exercising regularly, eating healthy, and taking care of yourself emotionally, then keep it up!

In conclusion, as a leader, you need to stay sharp in these three areas. As a creative, these things may not come naturally to you. It takes a level of self-discipline beyond the creative behaviors. If you're looking for an easy and simple way to start, I will discuss some tips and suggestions in the next chapter.

Chapter 19
Go Out and Play

Chad is the CEO of an agency. He has seven children. Amazingly, he and his wife have energy to spare.

"How does he do it?" I asked myself.

I had recently been laid off and was looking for a new job. Chad and I had met at a conference when we were both leading departments for different organizations. Chad offered me a job when he learned I was looking for work. He wanted me to start as soon as I could.

Since my layoff, I had been having health issues and needed to make some lifestyle changes. I supposed a new job with new challenges would be a good start.

As a new employee, I drove to Nashville and met Chad at the Gaylord Opryland Hotel and Conference Center. The same conference where we'd met years before was where we began our new working relationship.

If you've ever been to the Gaylord in Nashville, you know it is by no means easy to get around quickly. The hotel sprawls over acres of land with numerous levels, walkways, balconies, and skywalks over restaurants and an indoor lazy river.

Keeping up with Chad was exhausting. Several times I found myself having to stop to catch my breath. While briskly walking from one end of the hotel to the conference center, Chad would often look back and see me pausing for air.

"You okay?" he would ask.

"Yeah. This is good for me. Just give me a moment." And then we'd be off to the next meeting.

One evening in our hotel room, after a long day of meetings, I asked Chad what he did for exercise. How did he fit it into his schedule while owning a company and co-parenting seven children?

He gave me the regular dad answer, "I play basketball with my kids and coach some of them for cross-country..." He also shared he had been doing a high-intensity ten-minute morning workout.

Surprised, I asked, "Just ten minutes?!"

And that was when it hit me. It doesn't have to be a thirty- to sixty-minute cardiac-causing workout session like I had done in my younger days. You can start with something small and manageable. Somewhere with five to six feet of space at home or a hotel room. No huge expense like a longtime gym membership or a treadmill in the bedroom that would later become a clothes caddy. Baby steps to build momentum, strength, and endurance.

Baby steps.

Exercise Tips

Whether you're a man or woman, starting and maintaining an exercise regimen is a must. Of course, I have to add the disclaimer: You should always consult your physician before attempting or changing exercise and eating habits.

Do you get enough regular exercise? It's easy to let exercise slide. And that's the way it begins, right? A slow slide from activity to inactivity. From low stress to high stress. From in shape to out of shape.

As I was advancing in my career and taking on more responsibilities, I started to come into work earlier to stay on top of the project load and administrative duties. My exercise habits began taking a back seat. It was only after I lost my six-pack abs and noticed how easily I got winded on staircases that I began to notice my decline in personal health. As a new leader, I knew I needed to do something but wasn't quite sure what or where to begin.

After researching, reading, and talking to friends, leaders, and trainers, I learned a few helpful exercise tips. I want to share some of those here with you in hopes that you will find them beneficial, encouraging, and easy to not only start but maintain as well.

Exercise Tip 1: Set up a regular cadence

To keep your energy level up, doing metabolic exercises at least two times a week is a good start. It is better if you can do three to four times a week, but don't stress if you can only get in two. Remember, start small.

It is easier to make it consistent when access is easy. If your workplace has an exercise facility, utilize it. Need to go low-tech/low-cost at home? There are plenty of YouTube calisthenic or yoga videos with great beginner workouts. You might already have some kind of gaming system at home, so leverage that by buying an exercise-related game. You may find you have some sore muscles after getting back into an exercise routine. So be sure to space out a day or two in between exercising to allow yourself time to heal. The key is to make exercise fun and a regular part of your week.

Exercise Tip 2: Start with no or simple equipment

You don't need to break the bank on equipment. Buy some stretch bands, kettle bells, or dumbbells, and begin a series of exercises to tone your muscles, burn fat, and get in shape.

As noted above, if you already have a gaming system, use it for starting an exercise program. Get a friend or family member engaged as well. I have a cousin who does yoga with her elementary school-aged son by watching online videos. Calisthenics is using your own body weight. If you want more advanced calisthenics, there are plenty of options online. The key is to start with what you have and then, if you choose, add gear over time.

Exercise Tip 3: Begin with compound metabolic exercises

What is a compound exercise? It's an exercise that benefits several muscle groups at once and is not focused exclusively on any one. An example is a squat exercise which engages your legs, glutes, core, and lower back. Metabolic means getting your heart rate up while you are doing exercises with little rest in between. This can help maximize calorie burning. For examples of a ten-minute and forty-five-minute exercise routine, see the *Creatives Lead Companion Workbook.*

Nutritional Tips

With long days and sometimes long nights, plus travel, your diet can easily go astray. It is important for you to pay attention to your diet and eat as well as you can. Here are a few tips regarding your diet.

Nutritional Tip 1: Cut down on carbs and sugar

The western diet is often loaded with carbs and processed sugar. What you eat and how much go hand in hand with your health and exercise. I have a friend who loved Coca Cola® sodas. When he cut back, he lost ten pounds within a month. If you want to lose weight, first try cutting out carbs and processed sugar.

Nutritional Tip 2: Where to spend your money

Is eating healthy expensive? I talked to a nutritionist about the costs of eating healthy. I noted it could get quite expensive so I asked him, "If you had to spend money on one area, meat or veggies, what would it be?" He said spend your money on good quality meats: chicken, fish, and beef. Also, knowing what the animals were fed helps because you will be eating what they ate.

Nutritional Tip 3: Watch your portions

I am not advocating any certain diet like Keto, Vegetarian, Mediterranean or Plant Paradox®. That is up to you. I am advocating for balanced, healthy eating. Make sure your plate is half covered in veggies, while one quarter is protein, and the final quarter is a good slow-release carbohydrate like sweet potatoes, brown rice, or apples.[24] Also, the amount of food you eat should be in proportion to the amount of exercise you do. If you're exercising three times a week, your muscles will need the proper nutrients to heal. If your exercise slacks off, it can be easy to keep eating the same volume of food. This can lead to weight gain, so be sure to keep it in proportion.

Nutritional Tip 4: Meal prep can cut down on snacking

Why do I include meal prep? It is too easy to visit the cabinet or fridge when you're hungry and find junk-food to snack on. You may find yourself snacking several times a day. Your body is trying to tell you something—not just that it needs food, but it needs the proper food. This is where meal preparation can save you time and headaches (literally!).

Once again, there are plenty of resources online. Find what works for you, but keep it high protein, and your body won't be craving junk. For instance, I did an online search for "quick meal prep, high-protein lunches" and found these recipe ideas below:[25]

- Spicy shrimp bowls with edamame and avocado
- Mediterranean chicken and quinoa bowls
- Vegan Southwestern Buddha Bowls

Nutritional Tip 5: Minimize alcohol consumption

Finally, be careful with alcohol. Moderation is the key. There is a reason you have heard the term "beer belly." Too much alcohol can impact your weight, disrupt your regular sleep routine, it can dehydrate you, and can impair decision making. Below are a couple tips to take into consideration regarding alcohol:

- Keep the consumption down to no more than four to five drinks a week.
- Be sure to eat something when you drink—protein and veggies are a good choice.
- Include a glasses of water with your drinks to minimize dehydration.
- Do your best to keep the drinks low-carb and low sugar.

Track Your Progress

If you do not have a fitness or health-related tracker, it would be a good idea to invest in one. There are various kinds of technology, from wearables to apps, that can help you track your exercise, heart rate, rest, weight, medications, and nutrition. Many of these have social aspects where you can connect to friends and family for competition, inspiration, and accountability. Some apps and equipment offer subscriptions to routines and access to trainers and coaches. Take advantage of these as your budget allows and watch the improvements begin.

I hope you have found these tips helpful. As a leader it is important to stay healthy and take care of yourself. As a creative, it's one of the best things you can do for your career—Really!

Chapter 20
Mandatory Ping-Pong

I had lunch with my friend, Tim. It was great to see him and reconnect after many years. Afterward, we walked back to his workplace for a tour.

"How long have you been here?" I asked.

"Can you believe it's been ten years!"

"Wow! That's unheard of nowadays."

"I know, right? Jeff, the boss, is a great guy. He really takes an interest in people. He knows how hard we all work and he makes room for fun."

"What does that look like?" I wondered.

After the tour of his offices, two things stood out to me:

1. Everyone seemed genuinely engaged in what they were working on.

2. Everyone seemed genuinely happy and content.

To some of you who read this, my examinations may be commonplace. You have fun at your workplace as well. Yet, to others of you, this may be foreign and even a little bit envious. I would venture to guess that many of you fall into the latter group. You have never experienced a work environment where you were genuinely engaged, believed in what you worked for every day, and were emotionally happy and content to go to work.

Many people I talk to long for this kind of workplace. There are numerous studies that show the value of emotional health and fun in the workplace. My friend Alexander is on a crusade to promote "happy" workplaces. In his book, *Happy Hour is 9 to 5*, he notes that happy workplaces exhibit the following:

- Higher productivity—happy people achieve better results.
- Higher quality—because happy employees care about quality.
- Lower absenteeism—people actually want to go to work.
- Less stress and burnout—happy people are less prone to stress.
- The best people—people want to work for happy companies.
- Higher sales—happy people are the best salespeople.
- Higher customer satisfaction—happy employees are the best basis for good service.
- More creativity and innovation—happy people are more creative.
- More adaptability—happy people are much more adaptive and open to change.
- Better stock performance and higher profits—for all of the above reasons.

> Simply put: Happy companies are more efficient and make more money. And they make people happy, which is of course a goal in itself.[26]

So what can you do?

Well, you have a couple options: One is to look for this kind of organization that you can give yourself to—an organization that you appreciate and one that appreciates you! As a newly minted leader in your organization, I am going to assume you don't plan to leave anytime soon. So the other option is to create this kind of environment within your current workplace. Is it possible?

It's possible.

I have seen it. Granted, I have seen it in a handful of places, but those are becoming more prevalent. Get started today!

You might be asking, "How can I create an emotionally healthy and fun culture?" Here are some steps Alexander recommends you start on:[27]

First, get yourself happy.

Remember, your team takes their cues from you. If you're not happy at work, guess what? The team is not happy either. As you begin to lighten your mood, watch it spread.

Make time for your people.

One idea I have used and seen other leaders use as well is to have an "open office" time where anyone can come by to talk about anything: sports, work, family, fashion, you name it. We also discussed setting up team time and one-on-one time with employees. While these are certainly times to discuss work, they can also be times to see how happy your team is and solicit questions, ideas, or concerns.

How happy are your people?

Alexander suggests watching your team and creating a spreadsheet with each person listed. Create three columns, one for each person's *name*, next to that a *rating* column for how happy you think they are, and the third being your *reason* for the rating. He suggests watching them for several days and making any needed updates to your spreadsheet. Finally, he recommends meeting with the team one on one and sharing your results, asking them if they feel it is accurate. Why and why not? Lastly, ask them to rate you as a leader and share their reasons. Be open to any criticism, thank them, and then act on the feedback.

Visualize your happy organization.

This is a visualization exercise from which you will want to capture notes. What does a happy organization look like? What does it feel like? Take some time to think about the future of your team. What would a day look like in their shoes if they loved coming to work? Start from where they are about to leave for work and visualize the day to the point they return home and are asked how their day went. Capture those thoughts, dreams, and goals. Next, you'll develop cases for doing something. Imagine why the team/organization will be better when it's happy.

Create the business case for happiness at work.

Think about the different areas that impact your team. How would a team that is excited and energized impact communication, absenteeism, productivity, creativity, and quality? Now think about the time savings and subsequent cost savings. Are you getting the picture?

Put happiness first.

What are the priorities for your team? Is your answer a series of business goals and percentage increases? What if you were to flip that on its head and put your people and their happiness first? Here is what *Inc. Magazine* found out as the top five reasons Googlers like working for Google:[28]

1. Work that matters — "It's cool stuff that makes people happy."
2. Benefits for families — You can take 12 weeks of paternity and 22 weeks of maternity leave without hurting your career.
3. "Genius" co-workers — "The company attracts some of the best talent and best people to work with in the world..."
4. Smart perks — From the on-site doctors and haircutters to the gourmet cafeteria food, every perk at Google has a calculated reason, designed to keep employees satisfied.
5. Unparalleled career opportunities — "Opportunities for career growth, and tons of career development resources available..."

Are you willing to put happiness first? What do you think will happen if you don't? Have you already had people walk out the door because they weren't happy?

If you feel these steps are not in touch with your organization, or corporate culture, I say it depends on the level of influence and determination you have. Explore all your options. Wouldn't you rather get up excited about what you're doing for work rather than dragging your rear into a dull, lifeless job while waiting for the next best thing or retirement? If you are in a large organization, work with HR and facilities to see about bringing in a Foosball table. Heck, donate one if you can! Have an afternoon that you take the team to the movies, do something—anything to make work fun and engaging.

Let's go back to Tim's story for one last item. After the tour of his office, Tim told me their team was having a *mandatory* ping-pong tournament that day. Everyone was expected to play. You could choose from either singles or doubles ping-pong.

What do you think of that? Mandatory fun in the office!

Applications for Week 6

You want to prove yourself as a new leader but don't neglect a proper diet, rest, exercise, and emotional health.

Practical Applications

This week you have four items to begin applying:

1. Start a "To-Do/What I Did" journal.
2. Begin to clear out junk food.
3. Begin exercising regularly.
4. Think of ways to inject healthy fun into your culture.

Start a One-Week To-Do/What-I-Did Journal

The goal is to find the areas between what you *want to do* and what you *actually do* in regard to home/work-life balance, emotional health, physical exercise, a healthy diet, and rest.

Divide a page into two columns for each day. In the left heading, write the date and "To-Do's." In the right column heading, write "What I Did." At the bottom of each page, leave room for notes. Now, begin each day by capturing your to-do's and end each day by capturing what you actually did. In the notes section, record any observations you have about what you wanted to do and what you did.

For an example of this journal, turn the page.

Monday, 5th - To Do's	What I Did
9:00-10:00 a.m. meeting	9:00-10:00 a.m. meeting
10:00-11:00 a.m. admin work	10:00-10:30 a.m. Brett had an issue to discuss
11:30-12:00 p.m. one-on-one meeting with Jane	10:30-11:15 a.m. admin work incomplete
12:00-1:00 p.m. Lunch	11:15-11:30 a.m. prep for Jane's one on one
1:30-3:30 p.m. planning meeting	11:30 a.m. - 12:00 p.m. one-on-one meeting with Jane
	12:00-12:30 p.m. Lunch shortened
NOTES:	
Schedule looks tight	Unexpected mtg pushed everything

After one week, ask yourself these questions:

- Where did I find myself cheating time?
- What came easily, or what was hard for me?
- What do I need to do or change to become successful next week?

Dealing With Junk Food

Consider getting rid of the junk food you have around your home. You can do it all at once or a little at a time. The goal is to transition to a healthier diet and eating schedule over the weeks ahead.

Begin Exercising Regularly

This week had several examples to choose from. Pick one, pick a start date, and determine your weekly cadence. If you keep this up through the remainder of our weeks together, you will likely feel and look like a whole new person. (For a list of basic exercise plans, see the *Creatives Lead Companion Workbook.*)

Brainstorm Fun Things to Do With Your Team

What can you do to make work fun and emotionally healthy? Think of some ideas to begin implementing. Ask your friends in Human Resources and ask your team for ideas and suggestions. Below are a few things I have seen and done over the years:

- Once-a-month Happy Hour where everyone meets up after work at a fun restaurant
- Celebrate birthdays with cards and a cake
- Bring in a Corn Hole/Bean Bag Toss game
- Once-a-month board games in the afternoon
- Bring in a puzzle for the team to work on during spare times
- Once-a-month movie where the team goes to a matinee as a group
- Decorate your cube or desk
- Quarterly cookout at a park or someone's home who wants to host
- Afternoon scavenger hunt
- Baking contest
- Dress up for Halloween
- Christmas gift exchange

Creatives Lead

Part 3

Gettin' in the Groove

In this part we will discuss helping you and the team begin to normalize, maintain focus, collaborate, and build momentum.

Week Seven

Classic Over Trendy

Understand your personal leadership style. Don't get caught up in trendy, here-today and gone-tomorrow, leadership fads.

Week Eight

Pay Attention

Push for focus and remove distractions; be a buffer for your team.

Week Nine

The Only Way to Have a Friend Is to Be One

Be human, be real, be transparent.

Classic Over Trendy

This week you want to learn to understand your leadership style and how it affects the team and productivity.

- Trendy Management Styles
- In All Things Balance
- Leadership Styles
- How Leadership Styles Affect Productivity
- Week 7 Practical Applications

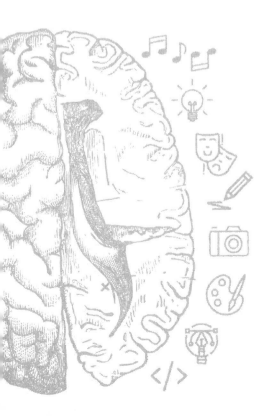

Chapter 21

Trendy Management

I used to have long hair.

I used to have a beard.

I used to wear skinny-leg jeans.

I used to wear bell-bottom jeans.

I used to play vinyl albums.

I used to play DVDs.

I used to wear thin ties.

I used to wear fat ties.

I used to wear my shirt tucked in.

I used to wear my shirt untucked.

I used to wear tennis shoes all the time.

I used to wear a tailored suit.

I used to wear thin-framed glasses.

I used to wear thick-framed glasses.

Notice anything about this list?

Every one of these used to be popular, fashionable—trendy. They fell out of style and now some of them are coming back! They come and they go. Are you like that personally—given over to trends? More important, is your leadership style like that?

We live in a world of planned obsolescence. Don't let your leadership reflect that idea. There are all kinds of trendy leadership techniques out there. The bookstore shelves are full of books on various leaders and how they turned a company around with their brand of leadership—and you need to mimic them. When I was a new leader, I read a lot of these kinds of books. Some of them were trash. Some of them were based on practice and common sense. My advice—stick with common sense.

Consider these leadership ideas:

- Treat people the way you want to be treated (see chapter 1).
- Be yourself.
- Know your limits.
- Know your strengths and play to them.
- Know your weaknesses and minimize them (hire people who are strong where you are weak - see chapter 11).

As the old saying goes, people don't care how much you know until they know how much you care. Do you care for your people?

"I do care for them," you might be saying to yourself. One way to find out—ask them. Try these questions—you may be surprised by the answers:

Do you feel that I care for you as an employee? That I am out for your best? If so, why? If not, why not?

Classics Never Fade

Have you ever heard of Dale Carnegie? Born in 1888, his parents were poor farmers in Maryville, Missouri. When Carnegie turned 16 years old, he joined his school debate team because he enjoyed public speaking. He went on to attend State Teachers College and graduated in 1908. After trying his hand at sales and acting, he gravitated back to public speaking and began teaching others. In 1936 his book, *How to Win Friends and Influence People*, was published. In 1955, Dale Carnegie died from Hodgkin's Disease at his home in New York.

Why do I share all this about man born in 1888? Because here was a leader who shared his success principles over 80 years ago, and guess what? They are still applicable today. They are classic!

Below are a number of the principles that Carnegie put forward years ago. See how many you can apply today:

- Don't criticize, condemn or complain.
- Give honest and sincere appreciation.
- Become genuinely interested in other people.
- Smile.
- Remember names.
- Be a good listener.
- Encourage others to talk about themselves.
- Talk in terms of the other person's interests.
- Make the other person feel important.
- Show respect for the other person's opinions.
- Never say, "You're wrong."
- If *you* are wrong, admit it quickly and emphatically.
- Get the other person saying "yes, yes" immediately.
- Let the other person do a great deal of the talking.
- Try honestly to see things from the other person's point of view.
- Be sympathetic with the other person's ideas and desires.
- Begin with praise and honest appreciation.
- Talk about your own mistakes before criticizing the other person.
- Ask questions instead of giving direct orders.
- Praise the slightest improvement and praise every improvement.
- Give the other person a fine reputation to live up to.
- Use encouragement.

Just because something is "old" doesn't mean it's no longer relevant. A principle is timeless. A technique can be a trendy fad.

I have an item in my closet that I've kept for years, and it's never gone out of style. It's my tuxedo. It's a classic. I have never had to replace it based on the event or the people I wore it around. It fits me. It was tailored to me.

Your leadership style should be the same. Be consistent no matter where you are or who you are around.

Be yourself. Be a classic!

Chapter 22

In All Things Balance

It was a cloudy Wednesday morning on August 7, 1974. New Yorkers were on their way to work. The World Trade Center was still undergoing construction and had many unoccupied floors. Passersby and those who did work in these historic buildings were treated to a site that at first astonished them, then had them murmuring, and finally applauding and cheering.

After six years of planning, Philippe Petit was taking a walk.[29] This walk was on a high wire between the two buildings, more than 1,300 feet in the air.

Before the rain started, Philippe made eight passes between the buildings as onlookers watched in amazement. Even officers that were dispatched to the roof cheered him on as it became apparent he was not getting down until his "show" was done.

As Philippe stepped off the wire waving to onlookers, he epitomized the word *balance*. Over the course of each pass between the towers, Philippe had to concentrate, focus on his goals, and make continual corrections to maintain his balance.

How's your balance?

This is one of those primary yet tough life principles for me. I have learned that I need others in my life to hold me accountable to this principle. Accountable to my dreams, goals, and aspirations as a businessman, father, and husband. What is this primary life principle? It is *balance*.

I can still hear Mr. Miyagi encouraging Daniel LaRusso in the movie, *The Karate Kid*, "Balance, Daniel-san, balance!" This has been made popular again in the series, *Cobra Kai*, where the grown-up Daniel says of himself, "Balance is my thing." Balance is something we all need because we're often torn between two directions, as illustrated below:[30]

Work	< >	Leisure
Action	< >	Meditation
Leading	< >	Following
Speaking	< >	Listening
Productivity	< >	Recreation
Serving	< >	Waiting
Giving	< >	Receiving
Applying	< >	Learning
Confidence	< >	Humility
Society	< >	Solitude
Duty	< >	Freedom
Joy	< >	Sorrow
External Life	< >	Internal Life

So how do you find balance? Is it appropriate or even possible in this day and age to find balance in life? With all the competing areas above, most people settle for focusing on one side or the other instead of finding the middle.

Sacrifice for the Sake of Excellence

Excelling in one area is good, right? Where would Michael Jordan or Warren Buffett be unless they excelled in one focused area? By no means am I suggesting we stoop to the level of mediocrity. Yet, while unbridled attention in one area may bring success, it almost always brings failures in another area. For example, "It is not uncommon to discover a physician who fails as a parent, an entertainer who fails as a spouse, a pastor who neglects personal health, or an executive who fails at all the other areas," says author and educator, Dr. Richard Swenson.[31]

The late Stanford physicist, Dr. Richard Bube, recommended a more balanced approach so that we do not fall into what he called "negative excellence."[32] A person who chooses to strive for high degrees of excellence in one or two areas often fails in others. While the person who chooses to live balanced has no outstanding levels of excellence, they *do not* have any areas of failure either.

There Is an Answer

You'll be glad to know that *life balance* is attainable. It starts with time. You thought I was going to say priorities. Business people practice prioritizing a lot. The mistake is, prioritizing dictates that one area is more important than another. What I am saying is that all these areas are important, and that to attain balance, we need to start with the time we give to each.

Learn to Say "No"

In today's Western society it is easy to overload and overbook ourselves. Saying "no" puts you in control of your time demands. This leads to the next item: Get better control of your life.

Important Over Urgent

Getting control means overthrowing the tyrannical rule of the urgent. Purposely reorient your life around the important, not the urgent, things of life. Urgent things will always pop up, but don't let them derail you from what's important in the long term.

Don't Focus on Weaknesses

Next, watch out for the circular trappings of trying to *find* the imbalance in your life. In doing so you run the risk of becoming even more unbalanced. Dr. George Rust warns, "We respond to our sense of imbalance by committing more time and energy to an area in which we feel deficient."[33]

The last thing you need to do is commit more time than necessary to a personal weakness.

Be Considerate

Finally, be considerate of others trying to live a balanced life. If someone tells you "no," learn to accept it. Just because we choose to overburden ourselves doesn't mean we have to do the same to others.

Balance is Attainable

Learning balance takes work, but it can be done. You might consider sharing your desire to live a balanced life with a close friend or peer and then ask them to hold you accountable. Give them permission to *ask you* how you're doing on a regular basis—and be honest in your reply.

Philippe Petit spent six years planning to traverse the height and distance between the towers in New York. He had the help of friends. He practiced regularly.

In the end, where did it get him? You might think he was thrown in jail or extradited, and you'd be wrong. All charges for trespassing were dropped, and he was required to give a show to children performing a high wire walk in Central Park—teaching a younger generation the art of balance.

In the next chapter, we will discuss finding out your primary leadership style. Here too, balance is imperative as your team begins to build momentum.

Chapter 23

Leadership Styles

"We need to leave the building now!"

I was a new designer working on our monthly publication. I was in the zone when my boss had jabbed her head into my office. "Huh, what?" I said looking up from my workstation. "Let me finish this one..."

"NOW!"

This was unlike Taylor. Normally, she was very easygoing. I was irritated that my work had been so rudely interrupted.

As I followed her out the side door of the building, I saw a large group forming at the far side of the parking lot. In the distance I heard sirens.

It was almost an hour later before we were let back into the building. There had been a bomb scare regarding a suspicious package delivered to our shipping department. In the end, it turned out to be a box of car parts an employee had had shipped to work, so he would not miss the package at home.

My original irritation at Taylor had subsided. I understood now why her approach had been so blunt and forceful.

Dictatorial, Authoritative, Consultative, Participative

One of the first leadership books a friend recommended I read was by Myron Rush. My friend was kind enough to let me read his copy. After I returned the book, I searched for a personal copy. On an obscure website, I finally found a used version that I purchased for my own library. While thumbing through it the other day, I was reminded of differing approaches to the use of authority.[34] Here is an excerpt and series of lists that I am sure you can relate to.

Leadership Styles

Definitions and descriptions of leadership styles range from the very simple to the very complex. Leadership styles can be identified by how authority is used, how a leader relates to others, how employees' minds and muscles are used, and how a leader communicates.

Dictatorial Style

The leader or manager using this style operates like a dictator. He or she makes all the decisions about what, where, when, why, how things are done, and who will do them. Employees failing to follow directions are usually severely disciplined or given cause for "early retirement" (as recently happened to a friend of mine).

The dictatorial leader traits are:

- All decision-making power is theirs
- Unrealistic in demands
- Uses excessive discipline and punishment
- Does not allow others to question decisions or authority

A more passive-aggressive version of this is:

- All decision-making power is theirs
- Unrealistic demands clouded in humor
- Subtle forms of discipline and punishment
- Allows questions about decisions (on the surface) but ignores them
  - Pretends to be your friend only to get their way

Authoritative Style

Because of the volatile nature of the dictatorial style, more leaders and managers opt for the authoritative style.

The authoritative leader traits are:

- Seldom lets others make decisions
- Feels they are the most qualified and experienced
- Considers their views to be most valid
- Lacks confidence in others' abilities
- Critical of differing opinions
- Rarely gives recognition
- Is easily offended
- Uses others for their benefit
- Action oriented
- Highly competitive

The biggest weakness of this style is the failure to recognize the skills and abilities within other people. Employees are often denied opportunities to use or exhibit their skills or decision-making. Yet, the strength of this style is to *produce action* when it is needed.

Consultative Style

This style focuses on using the skills, experiences, and ideas of others. However, the leader or manager using this style still retains the final decision-making power. To his or her credit, they will not make major decisions without first getting the input from those that will be affected.

The consultative leader traits are:

- Often involve others in problem solving
- Team building
- Retains right for final decisions
- Focuses their time on more important activities
- Provides proper recognition

- Delegates but keeps "veto power"
- Weighs all alternatives before final decision is made

Participative Style

A unique managerial style that many feel uncomfortable with is the participative style. Most of the authority, *not all,* is given to the team. The manager remains the team leader.

The participative leader traits are:

- Team member ideas are equal with the leader
- Everyone's input is considered
- Leader is team facilitator
- Leader is coach/player
- Frequently accepts team's ideas over own
- Focus is on stimulating creativity
- Creates culture of innovation

Is there a "right" leadership style?

Many managers tend to advocate one style over another. The fact is there is no "one-best-style" or leadership silver bullet. All the styles have some value. This may make you feel uncomfortable. You may be thinking, "That's not realistic!" or "I don't like causing conflict. Can't we all just get along?" The tension you are feeling is the difference between what is *real* and what is *ideal.* The reality is you may have to use all the styles listed above at one point or another. Ideally, as we discovered earlier in the book, you will land on a personal leadership style that fits your temperament. To put you at ease, let's discuss when and how to use each of the different styles.

Leadership Styles: When to Use Them

A question that is often asked is, "When? When do I use one style over another?" I have provided Rush's tips here for you to better understand when to use the dictatorial style over the consultative style or when to use the participative style over the authoritative style given the contexts and situations.

When the dictatorial style is appropriate:

- During emergencies or crisis
- When employee safety is at risk
- When severe disciplinary action needs to be taken

Keep in mind, the dictatorial style *is the exception*. Rush says it "should be used only in emergencies and on a temporary basis."[35]

When the authoritative style is appropriate:

- When new hires are unfamiliar with their jobs
- If there is constant misuse of authority
- When company rules are broken
- When you are the sole person responsible for a decision

When the consultative style is appropriate:

- When needing creative problem solving
- When conducting planning meetings for the team or department
- When training people for leadership roles
- When performing daily organizational tasks

When the participative style is appropriate:

- When you have a competent team
- In team or department planning meetings
- During team or department evaluation sessions
- When motivating top performers
- Any time you need innovative work
- When you need creativity

As you look through this list, you might be tempted to think, "I knew this." Yet, you might not be practicing what you intuitively already knew. There are definite consequences to your action or inaction as a leader. Take some time to look back through the styles and see what is appropriate for your team and environment.

Like Taylor, in the story above, you may find yourself resorting to a style that is not your norm because of the need at hand. Don't be afraid to use the style a situation calls for. Each leadership style has a unique impact, and in the next chapter, I'll talk about how these leadership styles affect team productivity.

Chapter 24

How Leadership Styles Affect Productivity

You may recall Jenn's frustration from the introduction to this book. Jenn had reported to me. Over time I had used the *participative style* of leadership to build an enthusiastic, engaged, and high-performing team. After I left the organization, there was a major change in leadership across several levels including the chief operating officer. The new COO was dictatorial in his style. The leaders underneath him waffled between dictatorial and authoritative in their approaches. I suspect this was primarily a way to "survive" in this newly toxic environment. The damage to the company and culture played out over a year. Morale tanked, there was often conflict, and employee fear ran rampant. The COO was removed a year later, but it was *too late*. Significant damage had been done, and the last I heard it had taken almost eight years to recover from one year under a poor leadership style! Let that sink in before we talk about how leadership styles affect a team.

Once more we will look at management consultant, Myron Rush, for insights into leadership styles—many of which you can find within most businesses or organizations around the world. As we learned in the last chapter, these styles are: dictatorial, authoritative, consultative, and participative.[36]

Each of the leadership styles has impact on reforming and/or creating team culture. There are both short- and long-term effects for each style. For instance, the authoritative style may produce tremendous results in a short amount of time. However, excessive use of authority will decrease productivity in the long term. People either get fed up and leave or fall into a malaise of hum-drum repetitive tasks without creativity and innovation.

All the while, a participative style may be unproductive in the short term. But the longer this style of leading, the more productive a team can become.

Many leaders never make it to a point of high productivity. They give up before the participative style kicks in and the team starts to perform. They see the initial drop in production and cannot wait long enough for the true results.

Do not give up.

Though many leaders and managers get discouraged seeing a drop in productivity when transitioning to a participative approach—productivity will come over time. Employees will see they have opportunities to create and innovate, and their production becomes greater than before.

Three Keys

There are three keys that determine your leadership style:

1.   How you view and use authority
2.   How you view and use Human Resources
3.   How you view and relate to people

The more you keep control, the more authoritative your style. The more you share control, the more participative your style of leadership. Rush says, "as a general rule, the more you move toward a participative team style, the more productive you and your people become."[37]

Questions for Reflection

Ask yourself these questions to see if you (or those around you) are moving toward a more authoritative or a more participative leadership style.

- Are employees involved in the planning process?
- What percentage of total employees knows the vision and goals for the team? The department? The company?
- Do employees feel ownership of their work?
- Do employees feel trusted?
- Is information readily exchanged between teams and departments?
- Is information received from others truly accurate?
- Is problem-solving delegated?
- Is there regular duplication of effort?
- Is there an inordinate amount of time spent correcting mistakes?
- Are relationships between leaders and subordinates good most all the time?
- Are team relations good most all the time?
- How rare is conflict?
- What is the company attitude toward authority?
- Are conflicts ignored?
- Do people fear failure?
- How do employees feel toward the organization?

I hope you find these helpful. I have found that when crises arise (and they invariably do), knowing the style of your boss or employees is invaluable to weathering the storm and coming out stronger on the other side. (Also, see chapter two.)

Applications for Week 7

As your team begins to normalize, you want to understand your leadership style. Don't be trendy or use gimmicks. How you lead impacts the productivity you are trying to build.

Practical Applications

After reading this chapter, you have only one item to do this week. Set aside time to do some soul-searching. Think about and answer the Self-Examination questions below.

Why a Personal Moral Inventory?

Every good leader I know, at least the ones worth following, take regular intervals of time for personal introspection. "Well, of course, that's a good business practice," you might say. Yet, rarely do people in leadership positions look at their moral compass—that thing inside them that guides their thoughts and, consequently, their actions throughout the months and years. Common sense tells us this would be a good exercise, but it sure is hard to put into practice, right?

Why is it hard? That is for *you* to answer.

Below I have listed several areas for introspection to encourage you along the way. Set aside some time and reflect on these. If you feel compelled, use your journal to capture your thoughts during this self-examination. It may be hard because you will not like what you see. That could imply a need for change, and change does not come easily, but it can have great rewards.

Self-Examination Areas

These questions for introspection can lead you to understand yourself better, keep a greater life balance, and be more purposeful about the type of creative leader you want to become.

Personal Life

- What consumes my thought life?
- Do I tend to lie? Why?
- What is the health of my relationships with family and friends?
- Do I respect the opposite sex?
- Do I want what is not mine? Why?
- Do I prefer lists or piles?
- Do I procrastinate? Why?
- Do I know my pet peeves?
- Am I organized or spontaneous?

Public Life

- How do I treat employees?
- How do I treat my peers?
- Do I talk too much?
- Am I a good listener? Why or why not?
- Do I have empathy?
- Do I care about those less fortunate than me?
- What do I think about when I consider needy people?
- Am I genuinely interested in my community?
- How do I use my money?

Emotional Life

- Am I short-tempered? Why?
- What is my attitude toward revenge?
- Am I a hospitable person?
- Do I tend to be optimistic or pessimistic? Why?
- In most things, what is my motivation?
- Am I jealous? Of whom? Why?

A few additional resources you may be interested in:

- *StrengthsFinder 2.0* by Tom Rath is an excellent resource for assessing your personal leadership strengths. Developed by Gallup, they uncovered thirty-four unique themes in leaders. Find out your top five. Buying a printed copy of the book gives you a code to take the online CliftonStrengths® assessment.

- *The Road Back to You: An Enneagram Journey to Self-Discovery* by Ian Morgan Cron and Suzanne Stabile. Enneagram is a personality typing system for discovering how you are wired, both positively and negatively.

Pay Attention

This week as you continue to build momentum, you will want to make sure you and your team do not get distracted. Staying focused on the *important* will keep you from getting sucked into the *urgent*.

- Focus
- Distractions
- The Power of Enthusiasm
- Week 8 Practical Applications

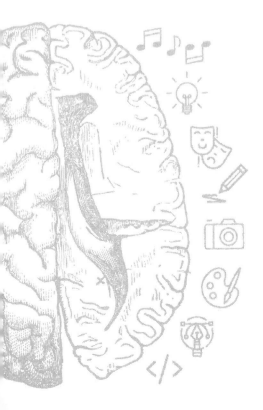

Chapter 25
Focus

In 1886, a pharmacist named John Pemberton invented the drink known as Coca-Cola®. Six years later, the Coca-Cola Company was founded. A year after that, Caleb Bradham invented the drink originally called "Brad's Drink." It was renamed Pepsi-Cola in 1898, and the cola wars were off and running.

Over the years, Coca-Cola has maintained its focus on investing in and selling beverages with one exception. In 1982 the Coca-Cola Company bought Columbia Pictures—later sold to Sony in 1989. PepsiCo®, founded in 1965, was due to a merger with Frito-Lay®. Unlike Coca-Cola, PepsiCo expanded its food and beverage products only to divest from many of them during 1997. Some of the brands spun off or sold included: Pizza Hut®, Taco Bell®, KFC®, California Pizza Kitchen®, D'Angelo Sandwich Shops®, Hot N' Now®, and Wilson Sporting Goods®.

Al Ries' book, *Focus: The Future of Your Company Depends On It*, was published in 1997 and chronicled the PepsiCo dilemma in chapter six titled, "A Tale of Two Colas."[38]

> It's not fast food that is slowing PepsiCo down. It's the fact that the company, for all its successes, is fundamentally unfocused.[39]

It makes you wonder if PepsiCo executives read Al's books and later divested of many of the brands I just mentioned. Unfortunately, *damage* had already been done. All the while, Coca-Cola maintained focus on the beverage market.

Ries went on to say,

> Perhaps the most important problem faced by an unfocused company like PepsiCo is that it competes with its customers. Instead of finding synergy in multiple product lines, most companies find the opposite: One of their product lines tends to undermine the other. In PepsiCo's case, their restaurant chains compete with their beverage prospects.[40]

Even though Ries' book came out in 1997, over ten years later a 2008 report from Beverage Digest stated PepsiCo's market share in the U.S. was 30.8% while Coca-Cola Company came in at 42.7%.[41] That is the power of focus.

In contrast, let's look at another company that had invested in numerous products and markets but turned the ship around in a very short time. Since ousted founder and CEO, Steve Jobs, Apple®, Inc. had been through three CEO's in a very short amount of time. John Sculley had been president of PepsiCo for six years before he became the CEO of Apple®. For almost ten and a half years, Sculley ran Apple. After Sculley came Michael Spindler who reigned for about two and a half years. During that time, several product lines were introduced: PowerPC, Newton, and Copland operating system. Spindler was ousted by Gil Amelio. Amelio cited several problems at Apple, including a shortage of cash and liquidity, low-quality products, lack of a viable operating system strategy, undisciplined corporate culture, and fragmentation in trying to do too much and in too many directions.[42] To address these problems, Amelio cut costs, reduced Apple's workforce by one-third, discontinued the Copland[43] operating system project, and oversaw the development of Mac OS 8.[44] Even with these changes, Amelio often urged the board to approve more and more products. Amelio's tenure was one and a half years before Steve Jobs returned, through a boardroom coup, and assumed control as interim CEO.

One of the first things Jobs did on his return was focus the company. "Deciding what *not* to do is as important as deciding what to do," Jobs said.[45] After looking at the dozens of versions of the Macintosh computers in production, Jobs had had enough. He went to a whiteboard and sketched a two-by-two chart. He labeled the columns "Consumer" and "Pro" and the rows "Desktop" and "Portable"—these would be the four products they would focus on making. Focus also meant getting Apple out of other businesses like personal digital assistants, printers, servers, and licensing its operating system. In Walter Isaacson's biography, *Steve Jobs*, Isaacson says this about the late founder:

> This ability to focus saved Apple. In his first year back, Jobs laid off more than three thousand people, which salvaged the company's balance sheet. 'We were less than ninety days from being insolvent,' [Jobs] recalled. At the January 1998 San Francisco Macworld, Jobs took the stage... he touted the new product strategy. And for the first time he ended the presentation with a phrase that he would make his signature coda: 'Oh, and one more thing...' This time the new 'one more thing' was profit. 'Think Profit.' When he said those words the crowd erupted in applause. After two years of staggering losses, Apple had enjoyed a profitable quarter, making $45 million. Jobs was back and so was Apple.[46]

Al Ries describes the value of corporate focus:

> The sun is a powerful source of energy. Every hour the sun washes the earth with billions of kilowatts of energy.... A laser is a weak source of energy. A laser takes a few watts of energy and focuses them in a coherent stream of light. But, with a laser you can drill a hole in a diamond or wipe out cancer.

> When you focus a company, you create the same effect. You create a powerful, laser-like ability to dominate a market. That's what focus is all about.

When a company becomes unfocused, it loses its power. It becomes a sun that dissipates its energy over too many products and too many markets.[47]

We have seen the effects of unfocused companies above and the long-term consequences. It takes great effort, resilience, and vision to focus. Just like your company needs focus to thrive, *you* and *your team* also need focus. You need to focus on your goals, the health of the team, and your personal time and attention.

Focus on the Goals

Your manager or director has provided you with goals for the quarter and possibly the year ahead. I hope this has been the result of several conversations in which you helped define the goals and accomplishments for yourself and your team. If not, I recommend getting clarity on these goals. Make sure they are the right goals and in priority order to support the company goals laid out for the year.

COMPANY GOALS

DIVISION GOALS

DEPARTMENT GOALS

TEAM GOALS

YOUR GOALS

Once you have your goals, get with your team to socialize them and get feedback on what will be needed to accomplish them. Are there any dependencies on other teams or departments that you will need to communicate with? The sooner you set up these meetings to refine and discuss, the better you will be able to focus yourself and your employees.

Print out these goals, display them somewhere for the team to see, and measure your progress against these goals weekly. Talk about your goals in your daily and weekly meetings. Doing these things will keep your goals front and center without distraction.

Focus on the Team

You are responsible for *your* team and not anyone else's. How is the team feeling? Are they stressed? Are they scattered over too many projects? You need to focus on the efforts and effectiveness of your team. Sometimes this means shielding them from other work, other teams, or other managers.

Have you ever said "no" to work?

"What?!" you may say, "I cannot do that."

Yes, saying *no* to work is sometimes necessary to keep your team healthy and effective. You know how much they can accomplish, and at times, you need to manage-up to the boss or director who likes to pile additional work on at a whim. Work for works-sake is not healthy. Having clear goals and priorities as mentioned above helps prevent unhealthy dynamics.

Shielding your team from other teams may be necessary as well. You are creating an environment with your team. You may know other managers who have created unhealthy environments with their teams. Do not let those bleed over into your team. One team's lack of preparation or overcommitment doesn't mean yours has to take up the slack or take on the burden. If another team's members are impacting your team negatively, you need to politely step in and protect your team. This could also mean coaching your team in how to effectively handle the offending party.

You are also a buffer for your team when it comes to other managers and leaders. You may receive legitimate feedback about the quality of your team's work or that of one of your employees from other managers. You choose how to handle the feedback. You know your team best and what's happening in their lives. The other leader does not know what is happening with your team and does not care. Be considerate of the flip-side as well—

you do not know the details of what is happening with other teams or their members. Show grace, but be willing to speak the truth when you need to.

As you're learning in this book, when you care for your people, they will care for you. Beating them with a leadership stick is not a long-term answer. You'll drive people away. Some bosses do this, but you won't. You're better than that. You need to focus on your team, so they can focus on their work.

Your Time and Attention

Finally, you will want to pay close attention to your time and where your attention is given. There will be many other people and projects trying to crowd out your calendar and draw your attention away from what is important. You must remember to give primary focus to your goals and to your team—that's what you'll be held accountable for at the end of the year. Not how many meetings you made or missed. Not how many presentations you gave. Not how many business trips you went on. All these are *good* things, but the *important* things are your goals and team. Don't allow yourself to get distracted by the good things. Focus on the important things. Like Steve Jobs said, "Deciding what *not* to do is as important as deciding what to do."

Next, we will discuss distractions in a little more detail. Since you are often barraged by distracting media and communications, you will want to eliminate short-term distractions that compete for your time.

Chapter 26
Distractions

I was excited about getting into work. I was a new manager with an open door policy. I wondered what the day would hold.

"Bye, Honey! Gotta head to the office. Full day today," I said as I ran out the door.

Traffic was a blur as I was processing in my mind everything I needed to do for the day. I parked at the back of the lot, so I could get a little exercise for the morning. As I walked down the hall toward my office, I saw several team members had already arrived and were busy at work.

I plopped my satchel down, said "good morning" to several employees, grabbed a cup of coffee, and sitting at my desk, turned on my laptop. I started looking at email when Tommy walked up to my desk.

"Can we talk for a minute?"

"Sure," I answered. "What's up?"

Twenty minutes later, Tommy left, and I got back to my email. My calendar reminder pinged to let me know my first meeting was in fifteen minutes.

"Shoot. Guess I'll have to catch up on email later. I need to prep for this meeting. What was it I needed to read before the meeting?" I looked at the agenda and followed the link to the document listed. Next thing I knew, I was scurrying off to my first meeting. While walking down the hall, I again thought of the things I needed to accomplish before the end of the day. "I should write those down," I thought as I sat at the meeting table. I jotted a few items on my paper pad as people filed into the room, and then the meeting was off and running.

Two hours later I was back at my desk. "Okay, what do I need to do now?" And so the rest of my day went—trying to get my work done between meetings, drop-ins, email, and catching up on documents sent to my attention.

Later that night, my wife asked, "How was your day?"

"Fine."

"Did you get everything done you needed to work on today?"

"Uh...." As I thought about my day, I realized it had totally gotten away from me. Of the five items I intended to get done, I only got one of them completed. How did I get so distracted?

Distractions. We all have them. Some we even create ourselves. Don't get distracted by good things, shiny things, trendy things. Stay focused on the right things.

Urgent Things?

There are lots of urgent things that can consume your work every day. A list of items include:

- Checking email first thing in the morning
- Building relationships with peers
- Building relationships further up the leadership chain
- Reading competitive research
- Reading about new trends in the market
- Staying on top of new technologies
- Organizing your desk
- Organizing your email inbox
- Catching up on old email
- Checking your company's intranet
- Taking online courses
- Reading reports

- Creating reports
- Watching presentations
- Creating presentations
- And more…

And, while all these are *good* things, these should not replace the *important* things on your to-do list or daily calendar. Urgent items should never become distractions from important items.

The Important Things

The right things to focus on have higher impact on you and the team, and longer term consequences. A list of these items for you and the team include:

Get in early and plan your day.

This is essential to avoid distractions throughout your day. Reviewing and planning your day based on your goals will help frame your mindset and set you up for success. Doing this first, and while you are fresh, will springboard you into your workday.

Get regular exercise.

As was discussed in previous chapters, exercise will give you the physical and emotional energy you need to be at peak performance. Distractions can drain your energy, so be sure to have high reserves by incorporating regular exercise into your week.

Create your daily to-do list and then prioritize.

Creating a To-Do list should be a practice you're already making into a habit. After putting your list together, prioritize it based on what you need to have completed by the end of the day in light of your goals. Then focus on your top items first.

Create a not-to-do list.

Creating a Not-to-Do list is something most leaders never do. This is something you should do weekly to assure you stick to your important tasks. Knowing ahead of time what you need *to do* and *not to do* will put you in the driver's seat and minimize distractions.

Establish focus time and breaks.

Throughout your day, you need both focused time and breaks. And I do not mean lunch breaks. Block your work time in twenty- to forty-minute increments and then allow yourself a ten-minute break before diving in again. This is based on the *Pomodoro* technique where you break down work into timed intervals with short breaks in between.[48] This has been proven to increase not only focus but also productivity.

Create meaningful meetings.

As you look at your time, you may notice most of it is wasted in meetings that are poorly run or not necessary. If you are creating meetings, make sure they are needed and efficient. Whether it is a daily stand-up, weekly project, or monthly strategic meeting, do this: Keep the time short and focused. Send out an agenda ahead of the meeting, notify the people presenting or sharing information to be prepared, and begin and end the meeting on time. Be respectful of other people. When your meetings do not end on time, they are either inefficient or you care more about yourself than others.

Track your goals.

This may seem like a no-brainer, but it is easy to turn around and wonder where the week or month has gone. Stay on top of your goals. Set time to regularly check your status in relation to your goals. This will help you in the long run. If you need to extend any deadlines, you should know well in advance.

Eat healthy.

A healthy diet and healthy snacks throughout the day can extend your energy level, keeping you sharp and focused. The midday slump will be a thing of the past as you power through your entire day.

Build up your team

We all need encouragement. If you're not getting it from your leadership, don't set that example for your team. Build them up! Think about each member on your team. What can you list that each person does well and should keep doing? What are they naturally good at? How do they benefit the team? Capture those items and make the time to speak life into your team members. You will be amazed how a simple note of encouragement can light a fire under an employee.

Empower your team.

Who doesn't want to feel empowered? You feel trusted that you can get the job done. What a great way to build up and motivate your team. Look for ways and opportunities to empower your employees every day. Let them make decisions and drive out the work. After all, you're building a high-performing team.

Review your day and learn from it.

This is key—at the end of your day, look back over what you accomplished and give yourself a pat on the back. Look at what you were unable to accomplish, and make notes as to why and how you can improve. Unless we learn from our mistakes, we are doomed to repeat them.

Have a hobby you enjoy at home.

You are home and need time to decompress. A hobby could be considered a necessary distraction. Why is this important? Because all work and no play makes Jane a dull girl. You need a healthy work-life balance and something to take your mind off the stresses of the day. For some it is exercise or dancing. For others it is reading or yard work. What creative outlets do you have that you can immerse yourself in and enjoy? Music?

Theatre? Drawing? Movies? You likely know what it is. Don't let your new role put your hobby in the back seat.

An interesting by-product of engaging in your hobby is that your subconscious can be processing work-related issues. You will find new ideas and solutions popping into your head simply because you are no longer worrying about them.

Spend quality *and* quantity time with the people you love.

Most people think quality time is all that is needed to maintain relationships. It's the depth of the time spent together some might argue. I say, it's both quality and quantity of time—especially when it comes to your family. You never know when your parent, sibling, spouse or child is suddenly willing to talk through what they have been thinking about or worrying over. You only get that by spending quantity *and* quality time together. Following this life principle will also keep you from getting distracted while at work.

Get plenty of rest.

It's the end of your day. You've fought the good fight. You've been focused at work and helped your team stay on track. You're knocking out professional and personal goals. It's time to get rest. We discussed the value of and need for rest in chapter eighteen. Let your mind and body get the rest they need, so you can start the next day early and refreshed.

If you forget any of these items listed, remember one thing—people come first. People are most important. Your immediate family first, your work team, your trusted friends and loved ones. Everything else can become a distraction. Put your focus on people first, and everything else will fall into order.

Chapter 27

The Power of Enthusiasm

The little boy sat in his school chair fidgeting. He didn't know why. He could not help himself. He just had a lot of energy. His teacher noticed him tapping again and called his attention to it.

"You need to stop tapping," she said, "before I have to send you to the principal's office?"

The little boy didn't want to go to the principal's office. He tried to stop tapping his hands, but sometimes he didn't even know he was making noise. It was not long, and he found himself tapping on the table. It was not intentional. He did not mean to be a distraction to his classmates, but his teacher was on her last straw.

"To the principal's office, young man!"

Head hung, the boy shuffled down the hall to the office. The principal looked up as the boy entered the room. After a few minutes' talk, the principal suggested the boy sit on his hands as a way to keep from annoying his classmates. The idea was good, but the practice did not last long.

While in another of his classes, the teacher caught him tapping his desk top and told the boy to stay after the dismissal bell. After the bell rang, the boy stayed in his chair wondering what trouble he was in this time. His teacher pulled out his desk drawer and said, "I have something for you." The boy walked around the desk as the man handed him a pair of wooden drum sticks. "Here, these are for you. You are not in trouble because I don't think you're a *problem*. I think you're a *drummer*."

Years later, as the boy reflects back on that pivotal event, he thinks about the impact that one person can have on a life. Now, the boy is a man. He stands on a stage speaking to hundreds of attendees. He's enthusiastic about his message. He has the crowd banging on plastic pails with drum sticks of their own. His enthusiasm is contagious. Who is this man? His name is Clint Pulver.[49] Maybe you've heard of him.

Clint is passionate about young people in the workforce. He's excited about what he does and wants to share his message with organizations large and small. His enthusiasm is infectious, and people leave his conferences recharged and ready to make a difference.

How about you? Are you excited about making a difference? Do you understand the power enthusiasm has on your team?

One of the questions I often ask speakers is, "Are you enthusiastic about your topic?" Whether it be a professional speaker, teacher, manager, or CEO, the power of enthusiasm has a remarkable effect on people. When you are enthused and excited about a topic or project, the people around you get excited too. When you are not enthusiastic about a topic or project—guess what? Yep, the people around you pick up on it and are not interested either.

The power of enthusiasm affects us all. Henry Ford said it well:

> You can do anything if you have enthusiasm. Enthusiasm is the yeast that makes your hopes rise to the stars. Enthusiasm is the spark in your eye, the swing in your gait, the grip of your hand, the irresistible surge of your will and your energy to execute your ideas. Enthusiasts are fighters, they have fortitude, they have staying qualities. Enthusiasm is at the bottom of all progress! With it there is accomplishment. Without it, there are only alibis.

Questions to Consider

Are you enthusiastic about...

- where you are in your career?
- the place that you work?

- the position you are in?
- your particular role on the leadership team?
- the projects you are working on?
- your personal and professional relationships?
- what you are studying?
- the direction your life is headed?
- what will happen today?
- what may happen tomorrow?

As you can see, enthusiasm touches most aspects of our lives. Don't settle for mediocrity. If you're in a place that you are less than enthused about, what options or opportunities do you see around you? Can you get excited about what you're doing? Do you need a change of *pace* or *place*?

Change of Pace

As the team begins to normalize, you should think about increasing their pace. As we touched on earlier, creative people can sometimes get in a rut. They need to be challenged to a new level. As you have gotten to know the team, you want to assess their individual and team capacity. Can they handle more? Can they move faster without sacrificing quality? It could be that a faster pace might be just what is needed to energize and excite the team—generating new enthusiasm about work. Be mindful not to swing the "pace pendulum" too far. If the pace is *always* fast, people can burn out. It is variety and a healthy change of pace that keep people engaged.

Another thing to consider is your personal pace. Do you feel driven? Do you push yourself each day? Is there a spring in your step and sense of urgency you're bringing to your work? If not, you should consider setting quick-turnaround goals for yourself to heighten your pace and inject some excitement back into work.

Change of Place

Some creatives like change. It promotes a sense of new possibilities. This can apply to your team and to you.

A change of place for your team could simply be allowing them to work from home one or two days a week. Your organization may already have policies in place about work from home so be sure to check those out. Many of the teams I have worked with enjoy the productivity and flexibility of working from home.

Along with work-from-home allowance, you could also look for a new place and space in the office to work. Creating a "war room" or team space in another area can help promote enthusiasm as well as team spirit.

Another Place All Together

I am not recommending leaving your current organization. You just moved into a new leadership role. Yet, like many creatives, you may thrive on change. New ideas, new problems to solve, new people, new things to learn, and new surroundings get you jazzed and enthusiastic. It could be you've gotten bored in your current work area, and another part of the organization looks interesting. Start researching that area or department. Meet people that work there, and ask them questions. Talk to your leadership and HR about opportunities to transition.

In some instances, you may feel you truly need to change companies. As you've been exposed to the senior leadership in your job, you may find it is combative and unhealthy. It could be dragging you down and impacting your physical and emotional health. If this is you, I recommend seeking the counsel of those who know you best and can offer objective advice. Be honest when assessing the situation. We can easily fool ourselves into thinking the company is worse than it actually is. As a friend once told me, the grass may look greener in the other yard, but it could be because of a leaky septic tank. Do you truly need to leave for your own health and sanity, or are you running away from a challenging environment? Getting honest and objective insight will help you with the decision-making process.

Life is and can be fun! Take a look around, assess the situation, and choose today what kind of enthusiasm you are going to show and teach your team. They will pick up on your cues whether excited or sour. Find something in your work, in each project, that *you* can get excited about. Make your excitement evident in how you talk and walk. Enthusiasm is a powerful thing.

Applications for Week 8

Focusing on important work and removing distractions for both you and the team are what we want to apply this week.

Practical Applications

This week you only have a few things to work on:

1. Priority Matrix.
2. Team Building Up worksheet.
3. To-Do, Not-To-Do, What I Did list.

Priority Matrix

There can often be a lot of churn at the leadership level as strategies and outcomes are being defined and implemented. There are also personality and political issues that will arise. A big part of your job is to shield your team from this churn so they can stay focused and productive.

Use the worksheet below as a template for both you and your team. You can work on this individually and as a team.

PRIORITY MATRIX	Urgent	Not Urgent
Important	Do first	Do later
Not Important	Delegate	Eliminate

Team Building Up Worksheet

Encouraging and being enthusiastic about your team provides the fuel that will help them get past most any issue. Use the worksheet below to capture information you can use to build the team up.

Employee Name:		
Naturally Does Well:	Very Good at:	How they benefit the team:
_____	_____	_____
_____	_____	_____
_____	_____	_____
_____	_____	_____
_____	_____	_____
_____	_____	_____
_____	_____	_____
_____	_____	_____
_____	_____	_____

To-Do, Not-To-Do, What I Did

Here we add the Not-To-Do column to our To-Do/What I Did tracking list. Track this over the next week and see how you can improve.

Date:		
Priority	To-Do	Not-To-Do	What I Did
_____	_____	_____
_____	_____	_____
_____	_____	_____
_____	_____	_____

The Only Way to Have a Friend Is to Be One

At this point you may begin to receive praise for your efforts. Don't let it go to your head. As you continue to move you and your team toward higher performance, you should be recognizing that nothing gets done without your friends. This week I provide a few cautionary tales of leaders who became self-absorbed and excluded their peers and friends. I continually tell new leaders: It is not about *you*.

- It's All About We
- Stop Covering Your A$$
- The Leadership Lone Ranger Is Dead
- Week 9 Practical Applications

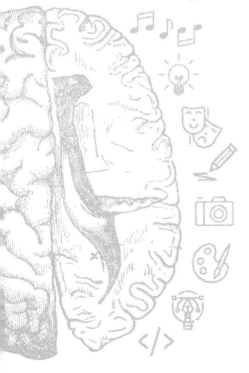

Chapter 28
It's All About We

Finn had recently been promoted to a leadership position. She was told to get the team leads together on a weekly basis to share their work and solve issues. Finn set up a reoccurring calendar event and invited all the team leads. The following week, the first meeting kicked off. As everyone gathered, Finn asked, "Who wants to go first?"

Crickets. No one quite knew what Finn expected.

Suddenly Eron spoke up. "I'll share what I have been working on," he said, using a common meeting app to share the screen on his laptop with the other attendees. As Eron was presenting, he noticed people were either scanning their own laptop screen or tapping away on their keyboard. It seemed that very few were paying attention. Eron was frustrated by this show of disregard but finished going over his work. Finally, he asked if anyone had any questions. No one did.

"Thank you, Eron, " Finn said. "Anyone else want to go next?"

Crickets.

This time Finn took control and called on the next person to present. The meeting was less of a collaborative problem-solving meeting and more of a litany of each person's weekly to-do list. Painfully, this went on until everyone had shared their work. It was a brutal meeting, and the lack of collaboration was palpable in the room.

As a new leader, Finn did not recognize that collaboration and teamwork, even amongst department leaders, did not come naturally.

Additionally, the lack of expectations and an agenda left attendees wondering what the meeting was trying to accomplish. Finn realized that teaching the group to truly collaborate would mean less about her position as a leader and more about the group functioning as a team.

Finn approached me the next day, asking for advice. I encouraged her not to be the bottleneck in trying to solve the issues. I also suggested she reach out to the attendees and spell out her expectations for the meeting and the group working together as a team. Lastly, I told her she should include an agenda as part of the meeting invite and appoint a facilitator and note-taker for each week. This would provide a sense of participation and ownership for the team.

In her book, *Mastering Collaboration: Making Working Together Less Painful and More Productive*, Gretchen Anderson states,[50]

> Collaboration doesn't come in one specific form and doesn't follow a recipe. It might be a set of people who are working independently on a common problem, sharing their work early and often to get feedback and test out ideas.

> Collaboration can take many forms, but at the core, it's a way to drive more innovative solutions to problems. ...We need to be careful not to start throwing "collaboration"at every cooperative situation, making things that should be straight forward into complex arguments, or inviting too many people into a co-creation space and slowing it down.

Finn needed to learn what collaboration was all about.

Transitions

We live in interesting times regarding our labor force. New generations of workers are entering the ranks. These workers are smart, tech savvy, and interested in collaborative environments where they can feel they are part of something bigger than themselves—part of a team.

All one has to do is look online or talk to high school and college students about the way they study and work on projects. It is highly creative and collaborative.

Anne Truitt Zelenka, author and owner of *Anne Zelenka – A Blog About the Connected Age*, writes about the difference between the "old Drucker mentality" of executive work and the "new Attention mentality" of web-related work.[51]

> Web workers do not start with their tasks or with their time. They start with their attention. And they do not start out with planning or by finding out where their time actually goes. They start by finding where their attention wanders, and what gives them energy and increased attention. Then they attempt to let their attention flow freely and to cut back on redundant or tired information sources that demand their attention without providing new ideas or insight. Finally they combine what they have found into something new (software, web design, industry analysis, etc.) and make it available on the web where it can earn attention itself and lead to an ongoing multiplication of attention.

Attention

Some of this thinking is similar to the *Attention Economy* mentality as discussed by Thomas Davenport and John Beck in the book of the same name. We all wrestle with what currently has our attention and what is vying for our attention. Then, we in turn crave attention—personal and vicarious attention.

In her article, Zelenka goes on to suggest that the web-based worker needs to expand his/her attention. It has been my observation that many have trouble expanding their attention. They get pulled off task and run down rabbit trails that lead to...what? Innovation and creativity? Or to something else attention grabbing?

If you are familiar with the practice of Design Thinking, then you likely have heard of *diverging* and *converging*. We diverge to do individual innovative work. For the creative, this allows them to multiply their attention. So we then need to converge to bring the attention back to focus on the problems we're trying to solve. Collaboration helps accomplish this.

Collaboration

I personally see a lot of value in the collaborative efforts of today's web-based workers. Yet, there needs to be a certain amount of discipline within these teams to become successful. Unlike Finn, at the beginning of this chapter, these team members hold each other accountable if any of them start to wander or stray too far. They dig for issues to resolve. They recognize they are co-owners and lay it all out on the table. There is power in this kind of collaboration.

Can there be unproductive time involved in collaboration? Gretchen Anderson says yes. If you are not addressing proper issues, the time can indeed be unproductive. She suggests collaboration when trying to:[52]

- Tame complexity - Bringing together a diverse group can help solve complex issues.
- Face ambiguity - Raising a trusted group to look at all the unknowns from various angles.
- Get alignment - Gaining buy-in from stakeholders that take part in the process.
- Engage employees - Solving complex issues as a team creates a sense of ownership.

It's All About Me

As you can tell, I am a big proponent of collaboration and teamwork. For me, collaboration cuts across internal and external business relationships.

Whenever I meet with someone, I am thinking, "How can we work together?" and "How can I help them succeed?" Unfortunately, the feelings are not always reciprocal.

I was introduced to a young businessman several years back when I was consulting. Although he appeared to be "sharp" and willing to collaborate on work opportunities, I got the distinct signals that this was "lip service" only. This proved to be true later on after repeated attempts to contact him. This man was only interested in relationships that furthered *his* agenda.

After reading the above incident, you may think, "He was only being intentional and purposeful in his relationships. Why engage in a collaborative relationship when there is no value?" To which I would say, if you are self-centered, then this statement is true. However, if you are others-centered, then every relationship has value.

Everyone deserves respect and courtesy. Simple responses like, "Sorry, I cannot get back to you—let's touch base in two weeks," or "Got your email—thanks," or "Now is not the best time to talk—can I call you back?" show respect. No response communicates that "you are not important."

Build Collaborative Coalitions

It is impossible to get work done within a vacuum. You and your team are part of a larger ecosystem with impacts and dependencies. Some of these partners who impact you are outside your organization, and many are inside. It is the same with the dependencies you have likely been experiencing. Most of these partners are outside of your control. That is why Michael Watkins says in his book, *The First 90 Days*:[53]

> Your success will depend on your ability to influence people outside your direct line of control. Supportive alliances, both internal and external, will be necessary to achieve your goals. You should therefore start right away to identify those whose support is essential for your success and to figure out how to line them up on your side.

I hope you learn, like Finn did, that as a new leader you do not have to present yourself as always in control. Don't set up the false expectation that you have all the answers. Praise your team and empower them. Create new teams that you can collaborate with on strategic issues. Build coalitions across your organization so everyone succeeds.

What will it take for you to move from "it's all about me" to "it's all about we"?

Chapter 29

Stop Covering Your A$$

The new COO began his first week by firing most of the directors. This sent a shockwave throughout the organization, and it soon became a dog-eat-dog mindset within the leadership team. Everyone was out for themselves. The prospect of looking for a new job was daunting under the current economy. Unfortunately, the remaining leadership team devolved into a CYA (Cover Your A$$) mentality.

When Ahn's directors came to him asking if their jobs were on the line, Ahn was noncommittal but said everything was going to be alright. It was later, during a series of one-on-one meetings, that each director was asked a series of questions—questions hinting that, if you did not support the new regime, your head was on the chopping block.

Backbiting and infighting among the vice presidents ensued as each tried to prove value and worth to the new COO. In the end, this sad CYA mentality did little good. Many of the leaders were discarded over the subsequent year under a variety of pretenses.

Don't Become a CYA Leader

The example above was an extreme situation, yet the CYA mentality permeates many businesses around the world. There seems to be an unspoken rule in the workplace: Look out for *you* because you're the only one *you* can depend on. From the corporate mission to the line-level employee, this idea infuses many organizations.

Some of this has been the backlash of "doing business" as some higher-ups say, while some has been the advance of technology. Radio host and business coach Dan Miller in his book *48 Days to the Work You Love: Preparing for the New Normal*, states this:[54]

> From 1920 until the mid-80's, getting a job with a large company was the dream of most every young American. The unwritten agreement between the corporation and the employee was, If you work for us throughout your working lifetime, we will take care of you.
>
> In the 1980s this unspoken contract disintegrated. Twenty million blue-collar workers, many of whom had spent their entire lives working for one organization, were let go. ...Today the average length of a job in America is 3.2 years. That means that in a 45-year working span, a person can be expected to have 14 to 16 different jobs.

No wonder most people are out for themselves. How much of this disloyalty have companies brought on themselves? Poor management drives employees to "watch their backs" so they do not lose their jobs. Poor leadership drives managers to "suck up" to leaders they do not like or respect so they won't lose their position of status and control.

As I mentioned in another chapter ("The Power Principle"), the illusion of being in control is just that—an illusion. There are forces outside our control that can and have direct impact on us as individuals and workers.

Man (or Woman) in the Mirror

So what kind of leader are you going to become? Are you interested in only yourself? Only interested in furthering your career agenda at the sake of others? Are you all about climbing the ladder of success? Do you have relationships only with those people you can use to further your leadership goals?

A day may be coming when you wish you had teammates around you. People who challenge you, care about you, and work *with* you—not *for* you.

Rafiki, the shrewd baboon from Disney's *The Lion King,* had wise words when he confronted Simba about his self-centered actions. Simba had run from his past. Dealing with the fallout from his previous poor decisions would not be easy. It would be painful. But Rafiki pressed Simba, asking, "So, what are you going to do?" Good question for us all.

So What Are We to Do?

How are we to break free from this mindset and be the leaders our teams want and need? Below I have outlined a few places to start.

Be Real

Don't try to be someone other than who you are. You have personal strengths and weaknesses. Don't try to hide weaknesses either. The truth is, you are no good at hiding them, and people know it already, which leads to the next point.

Be Honest

This seems to be a popular notion, but no one wants to be first. Be honest with yourself and with others. A reputation of honesty will get you far in life.

Be Accountable

Proactively seek out others within and without the company to hold you accountable. A work-life unexamined is a life that is headed for tough times. Invite trusted people into your work-life that will hold you responsible.

Be Ready

People are not going to like what you are doing. You will no doubt expose the insecurities and political posturing of others. Be ready for criticism and be ready to look for another place of employment if you're accused of rocking the boat too much. Popularity, while nice to have, is not the litmus test for good leadership.

When people see you for who you really are, they will admire you and be more trusting. They will not have to wonder if there are any hidden agendas. They will know you care about their success and not just your own.

Think about your current relationships, personal and business. Are you more interested in covering your a$$ or serving the team? The truth can be painful. So what are you going to do?

Chapter 30

The Leadership Lone Ranger Is Dead

Aria had a hard time getting along with her peer, Deane. As department directors, Aria knew they needed to work together, but Deane never seemed willing to collaborate. Not only was Deane unresponsive, but he always seemed to have his own agenda as well, and he had made it clear to others that he should be running Aria's department. He had the reputation of being a leadership *Lone Ranger*.

While this certainly frustrated Aria and made her job challenging, she was determined to reach out to Deane and try to build a bridge. Many of their projects overlapped, and Aria's team maintained a growing distribution channel for Deane's content. She asked Deane to join her for lunch off-site the following week. Surprisingly, Deane agreed. "Promising," Aria thought as she hung up the phone. However, lunch turned out to be anything but promising.

During lunch, Aria tried to get to know Deane on a more personal level, asking him about his previous work, family, and interests. As they discussed work, Aria breached the subject of their current relationship.

"Deane, from my perspective, it feels like there is no interest in working with me or my team. Many of our projects overlap but when I try to reach out, I don't get a response. It feels like there's a communication blackout. Am I reading that right, or am I off base?"

To Aria's astonishment, Deane stated that he didn't think Aria was needed, and that his department should absorb Aria's. Deane felt he should be in charge, and that he could do both jobs better. Needless to say, the lunch ended awkwardly, and no bridges were built. Deane clearly felt he was infallible, liked to be in control, didn't trust others outside his area, and did not like to relinquish any sense of authority.

Do any of these qualities sound familiar?

"Hi-yo, Silver...!"

Masked, dressed in grey, and riding a white stallion, the Lone Ranger was feared by all evil-doers. He was the only man that could save the day. If you were on his side, you had nothing to fear. If you were not on his side, you were either dead or imprisoned. His catch phrase was "Hi-yo, Silver, away! " as he and his steed Silver rode off into the sunset. [55] What started as a radio series in January 1933 later became a hit TV show in 1949. Regrettably, the Lone Ranger's time on TV came to an end, but his memory lives on.

In today's business world, Lone Rangers abound (and they are still dressed in grey–business suits). At times they are praised as talented independents, determined, and the kind of people who get things done. If you are on their side, you love them. You turn a blind eye to the wake of bodies and the dysfunctional relationships they leave behind. If you are not on their side, you may be in their sights.

A Lone Ranger may start out in an organization as "the golden child"— the one who can do no wrong and receives excessive praise. After two to four years, the gold starts to wear off, and lead shows underneath. The self-reliant attitude starts to compromise organizational cohesiveness. There is no inter-departmental teamwork–you're either on the Lone Ranger's team, or you're not. And don't even think about communicating with them. They prefer to keep to their agenda and will give information only if it suits their need.

Unwittingly, these kinds of leaders breed mini Lone Rangers on their teams. Interactions become combative with a my-way-or-the-highway mindset that could drive you to drink, leave, or seek counseling.

Can the Lone Ranger Survive?

Today's business landscape is changing and evolving at the same time. The pace of doing business means thinking globally–that is organizationally as well as internationally. A Lone Ranger cannot be off doing his/her own thing without accountability or consideration of the rest of the company. There are immediate and long-term consequences that are devastating. And here's where a concept foreign to the Lone Ranger comes into play: teamwork. Not just teamwork in their area (vertically) but teamwork across the organization (horizontally).

Pat Lencioni said it best, "Teamwork remains the one sustainable competitive advantage that has been largely untapped."[56] This means no one person is as good as all of us working together. This principle, though known, often goes unapplied. Teams bring differing perspectives, talents, and skills. Teams breed trust and synergy. Teams share work and accountability. Teams get things done thinking globally. While Lone Rangers would rather be off on their own, doing their own thing, their own way, and with their own people, this mindset cannot survive.

Develop a Growth Mindset

You may have heard of a fixed mindset versus a growth mindset. In her book, *Mindset: The New Psychology of Success*, Dr. Carol Dweck shares how nearly every human endeavor can be influenced by how we think about our skills, abilities, and natural talents. People with a fixed mindset are stuck and threatened, unable to take criticism or feedback. People with a growth mindset move forward, receive criticism, and are continuous learners.

See the lists below to determine where you need to develop: [57]

Fixed Mindset	Growth Mindset
Avoids challenges	Views challenges as opportunities
Shies away from things unknown	Acknowledges and embraces weaknesses
Unable to handle criticism or feedback	Learns to give and receive constructive criticism
Intelligence and talent is static and does not develop post birth	Intelligence and talent is dynamic and ever-improving
Does not carry out any actions without seeking approval	Prioritizes learning over seeking approval
Focuses on proving yourself	Focuses on the process instead of the end result
Threatened by the success of others	Inspired by the success of others
Regards effort as unfruitful	Thinks of learning as "brain training"
Understands failure as the limit of ability	Understands failure as an opportunity to grow
Gives up easily	Persists in the face of setbacks

On December 28, 1999, Clayton Moore, the man who played the Lone Ranger on television, died, and an era came to a close. So too is the fate of today's leadership "Lone Ranger." They are a dying breed and rightly so.

Yes, But What About Tonto?

An interesting fact should be noted on this topic. The writers of the original radio program recognized the Lone Ranger's *need* for a collaborator. The character of *Tonto* was introduced in the eleventh episode of the radio program. On the television series, Tonto was portrayed as a helpful friend and partner by the Canadian actor, Jay Silverheels.

Heroes and leaders throughout history have had in some form or fashion a partner or trusted confidant. We intuitively know we do better when working *with* others rather than working alone. Don't let yourself or anyone on your team fall into this trap. Reach out. Be intentional and build bridges vertically and horizontally in your organization. Be known as a collaborator and not a Lone Ranger.

Applications for Week 9

You're successful, and you are going to see greater success and that's okay. Yet, watch the trappings of self-centeredness. Remember how you got here. Yes, you've worked hard, but so has the team you lead. Be human, be real, and be transparent.

Practical Applications

This week was meant as a reality check. Here are a couple exercises to help you remember how you got to where you are today.

1. Identify your go-to people.
2. Thank You cards.

My Go-To People

Make a list of your go-to people. Those people you have gone to over the years for advice, mentoring, and plain old sanity checks. Those people who have been your cheerleaders, who have taught you and encouraged you in your career.

Next, set up time on your calendar, if you do not already meet with some of these people, and schedule time to meet. If possible, set up time over the year ahead. These people can be a lifeline throughout your career.

I have found we all need the following list of people in our lives. One person may fit several of these roles, or you may desire to have an expert in each area—you decide.

Kinds of Go-To People:

- *Mentor* - that person who is further down the road, has integrity, and is successful

- *Encourager* - that person who is your cheerleader and believes in you wholeheartedly
- *Mentee* - that person you can pour your life back into and share lessons learned
- *Counselor* - that person you can talk with about life and work-related problems, no matter how large or small
- *Old Friend* - that person who knows you best and has been with you through thick and thin
- *New Friend* - that person with whom you have interests in common and who provides a new perspective
- *Role Model* - that person whom you aspire to be like, whether it be as a friend, parent, leader, etc.
- *Truth-Teller* - that person who tells you the brutal truth because you both know it's best for you

Thank You Cards

Buy a pack of thank-you cards and handwrite, yes handwrite, then deliver a note of thanks and appreciation to each of your go-to people. This may seem like a simple or unnecessary thing, and you could choose to ignore doing it. You may also think, "I can just send an email or note on social media," but do not. To be the leader you want to be and the leader your team needs, I highly recommend doing this exercise. If you do, you'll find it not only rewarding—you'll find it revealing as well. And, it will pay off in huge dividends.

Part 4

Now You Try It

In this last part we will focus on creating long-term culture, thinking ahead, and building future success for you and the team.

Week Ten

It's Nice to Share

Understanding business finances, being generous, and giving yourself away are the topics for this week. These three simple practices can set up your team culture for a future of high achievement.

Week Eleven

I Answered That Question

Don't create a "fear of failure" culture—fail fast, learn, and keep moving forward are the focus for this week. You have a team of high performers. Treat them accordingly.

Week Twelve

You're So Creative

Creativity is a secret to success. No matter what you approach in life, approach it from a creative perspective. Whether it be working remote, injecting fun into the workplace, or taking time off to recharge—use it as a creative exercise and keep building for the future.

Creatives Lead

Week 10
It's Nice to Share

This week you will learn some accounting basics to help you through your administrative tasks. You will also learn that being generous with your time and influence, and giving back to your team, is always an investment in your future as well as theirs.

- Sharpening Your Pencil
- The Power Principle
- Replace Yourself
- Week 10 Practical Applications

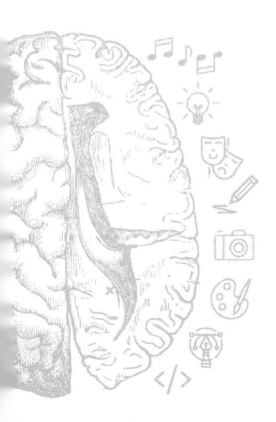

Chapter 31

Sharpening Your Pencil

"What the heck am I looking at?" I said to myself.

I was a brand new leader. This particular morning I was sent a spreadsheet to review. I had never seen so many tabs and formulas attached to a single spreadsheet in my life. I need to be careful, I thought, not to change anything in a way that would cause the other page calculations to break.

As I looked over my $6 million budget for the year, I knew I wanted to allow for salary and merit increases, travel and training, and new product development. I was told to allocate my budget to the dollar. This included operational expenses for a studio and library we maintained as well as all the office equipment and upgrades.

"Not exactly what I signed up for," I said to myself. Needless to say, the first time I tackled this aspect of leadership it took me almost all day.

Welcome to the world known as "Administrivia." It is a world of documentation, reviews, sign-offs, approvals, budgets, profits and losses, and more. It is not fun but it is necessary. As a creative, you are rarely prepared for the world of Administrivia. I would be doing you a disservice if I did not help orient you to your new surroundings. So follow me along the narrow path, lined with red tape, as I share some unique aspects of this world.

The Business Landscape

If you had gone back to school for an advanced degree, you might have considered a master of business administration, more commonly known as an MBA. For those desirous of climbing the leadership ladder, an MBA was the common track in higher education. As an MBA student, you would have covered some of the following material:

Human Resources	Organizational Behavior	Leadership and Team Building
Ethics	Accounting and Finance	Quantitative Analysis
Strategy	Operations	Economics
Negotiating	Business Law	Marketing
Management Information Systems	E-commerce	Communications and Presentations

At this point in your career you may have interacted with many of these functional areas or participated without knowing. Analysis, management information systems, team building, communications, presentations, and marketing are among the more common.

In this book we have covered much in the way of Human Resources, behavior, and leadership. However, in your new role you will be dealing with accounting and finance much more than you ever have. Depending on the size of the organization you are working for, you may be exposed to more or less financial documentation than someone in the same role, at another company. Below, I'll do my best to give you an overview of accounting, budgeting, planning, and alignment so you are not a total neophyte.

Accounting and Finance

Every organization has to keep track of the monies flowing within them. The responsibilities of the accounting and finance areas within your organization may include: [58]

Operations - payroll, cash disbursement, collecting cash, and
purchasing.

External Reports - statements created in line with generally accepted
accounting principles or GAAP.

Taxes - these include federal, state, property, sales, and payroll taxes.

Management Decisions - analysis and measuring of cash performance
to make decisions and set goals.

Transactions - this is a daily record of all sales, receipts, and spending
of cash.

Debits and Credits - an up-to-date record of accounts payable and
receivable and other accounts.

Making Adjustments - adjustments allow for items like bad debt,
accrued interest or taxes that don't get recorded.

Closing the Books - all profits, losses, revenue, and expenses are
accounted for and brought to zero balance before each new
accounting cycle.

Financial Statements - reports like income statements, cash flow,
balance sheets, and others that summarize all the activity
for that end of a business period.

A challenge in budgeting can relate to your project methodology. If you
are using project management to scope and schedule your projects,
budgeting is much easier. However, more organizations offering technology-
based services are opting for Agile as a methodology for managing projects.
Agile does not follow a typical project management flow or documents like
Gantt charts. While project management leans heavily on processes,
documentation, planning, and an approval process, Agile values interactions,
working software, collaboration, and responding to change.

The Project Management Institute (PMI) has several interesting
articles on the topic. Organizations that move to Agile methodologies have a
couple accounting challenges:

First, there is a difference in the completeness of requirements
defined up front compared to traditional, phased
development. Second, in traditional, phased development, the

preliminary phase, the application development phase, and the post-implementation phase are distinct. In an Agile project, it may be hard to disentangle some of the application development and post-implementation phases.[59]

My recommendation is to work with your accounting and finance team. Learn how they are measuring and budgeting for Agile projects, and that will give you a better idea of how to manage the numbers.

3 Financial Statements

I want to give a very brief review of the top three financial statements you may encounter and how to read them. The statements are the balance sheet, the income statement, and the statement of cash flows.

Balance Sheet

The balance sheet typically has the following three components: assets, liabilities, and owner's equity. These break down in the following ways.

Assets - resources owned for the future well-being of the organization. Cash, inventory, equipment, receivables, and buildings are examples of these resources.

Liabilities - financial onus to repay borrowing, debts, and other agreements to provide goods and services. Advances, bank debt, payables, taxes, and wages are examples of liabilities.

Owner's Equity - the accumulated financial measure of the investment in the company by the owner. Examples include common stock or other investments by owners and retained earnings (reinvestment of earnings).

Below I will use a fictional agency—Billie's Creative Services. A balance statement should equal out at the bottom of the statement. Notice the two columns below for Billie's balance sheet example:

Billie's Creative Services

Somewheresville, Connecticut
Balance Sheet
as of Date

ASSETS		LIABILITIES	
Current Assets		**Current Liabilities**	
Cash	$ 10,000	Accounts Payable	$ 1,910
Accounts Receivable	150,000	Wages Payable	50,000
Inventory	100	Taxes Payable	2000
Total Current Assets	$ 160,100	Total Current Liabilities	$ 53,910
Long-term Assets		**Long-term Debts**	
Equipment	$ 19,000		
less one year's.		Bank Debt	$ 10,000
Accumulated Depreciation	190	Total Liabilities	$ 63,910
Net Longterm Assets	$ 18,810		
		OWNER'S EQUITY	
		Common Stock issued	$ 100,000
		Retained Earnings	15,000
		Total Owners' Equity	$ 115,000
Total Assets	**$ 178,910**	**Total Liabilities + Owner's Equity**	**$ 178,910**

Income Statement

The income statement shows the "flow" of activity and transactions over a specific period of time. That period may be a month, a quarter, or a year. There are *revenues* from sales and *expenses* relating to those revenues.[60]

The equation to remember is: Revenue - Expenses = Income

Below I will use our fictional agency again—Billie's Creative Services. Notice the Gross Margin line. Have you ever wondered what *gross margin* is? In essence, gross margin is the income a company possesses after incurring the costs associated with producing the goods and services it furnishes. The *net income* at the bottom is the money a company profits after all expenses are deducted. An income statement for Billie's could look like this for the end of the year:

Billie's Creative Services
Somewheresville, Connecticut
Income Statement
for End of Year - Date

Sales to customers	$ 1,500,000	**$1,000,000**
Cost of Goods/Service Sold	500,000	
Gross Margin		
Less: Sales, General, and Administrative Expenses		
Payroll	$ 600,000	
Rent	100,000	
Utilities	50,000	$777,400
Marketing	20,000	
Cost of Equipment	2,400	
Other	5,000	

Operating Income		$ 222,600
Less Interest Expense		1,000
Income Before Taxes		$ 221,600
Less Fed and State Income Taxes		67,000
Net Income		$154,600

Cash Flow Statement

The cash flow statement uses the balance and income statements to paint a picture of the organization's health. According to author Steven Silbiger, this statement answers the following questions:

- What are the relationship between cash flow and earnings?
- How are dividends financed?
- How are debts paid off?
- How is the cash generated by operations used?
- Are management's stated financial policies reflected on the cash flow?

By using a statement of cash flows, managers can plan and manage their cash sources and needs from three types of business activities:[61]

1. Operations Activities
2. Investing Activities
3. Financing Activities

Once more I will use Billie's as our example.

Billie's Creative Services
Somewheresville, Connecticut
Cash Flow Statement
for End of Year - Date

OPERATING ACTIVITIES		
Net Income		$ 154,600
Add back expenses not using cash: Depreciation (Allocated cost of equipment)		3,000
Adjust for changes in workplace capital: Increases and decreases during the year		$ 157,600
Current Assets: Customer receivables (increase) decrease	-$100,000	
Current Liabilities: Vendor payable (increase) decrease Wages payable (increase) decrease Taxes payable (increase) decrease	(80,000) (5,000) (2,000)	$13,000
Cash Flow from Operating Activities		$144,600
INVESTING ACTIVITIES		
Purchase of equipment	-$30,000	

Cash Flow from Investing Activities		-$30,000
FINANCING ACTIVITIES		
Proceeds from Bank borrowing	$ 10,000	
Sales of Stock to Owners	15,000	
Payment of Dividends to Owners	0	
Cash Flow from Financing Activities		$25,000
INCREASE IN CASH FOR THE YEAR		**$5,000**
Cash at the beginning of the year		0
Cash at the end of the year		$ 5,000

After looking at this example, you might still be wondering, why is the cash flow statement important? It helps to see the truth of the financial situation. If an organization seems profitable but is borrowing large sums of money to stay alive, there is an issue, and you will see it in this statement. If something is out of balance between operations and year-end cash, you will see it here and can begin to solve the problems.

For most creatives, finances is *not fun*. That's okay. As stated earlier, get to know your finance department, CFO, or accountant. While it is not exciting, it is an essential part of being a good leader.

Budgeting

When it comes to budgeting for your team or department, you will likely have two choices: 1) estimating what you will need for the year and then making a case for the final amount, or 2) being given a predetermined amount and then allocating your monies accordingly. Below are some of the items you will want to consider budgeting for if they are not already specified:

> *Internal staff* - this will likely be the largest part of your budget. Make allowances for annual increases, merit increases, one-time rewards, and potential new hires.
>
> *External labor* - if you use contractors, this may be easier to calculate since they have assessed the costs of their services already. Don't discount the opportunity to negotiate their rates if you feel they are too high.
>
> *Equipment* - you will need to factor in the use of your current equipment, any new equipment, any updates or upgrades, as well as any equipment needs for your contractors.
>
> *Materials* - these costs can vary (e.g. from lumber to software) depending on the nature of what you do and what your organization does.
>
> *Training* - this may include conferences, online training, books and subscriptions, as well as your regular off-site planning meetings.
>
> *Travel* - this will usually include flights, rental vehicles, lodging, and meals.

Doing the Right Things

Having had my own company, I tend to take an entrepreneurial approach to leadership, no matter what environment I find myself in. While this work approach has come second nature to me, I first saw it in print in 2011 with Dave Ramsey's book, *EntreLeadership*. Dave wanted to grow leaders, but not just your everyday garden-variety leader. He wanted leaders with an entrepreneurial bent to infuse the DNA of his growing company. Dave puts it like this:

As I thought about what a pure entrepreneur is, I decided in three seconds I didn't want to grow a company full of us. Leading that group would be like herding cats or trying to nail Jell-O to a tree. I do want the spirit of the entrepreneur woven into our cultural DNA, but a whole building full of us would be a really bad plan.

So growing leaders was too refined and calm for me, but growing entrepreneurs was too wild and chaotic for me. So I decided we needed to grow a combination of the two... and thus the EntreLeader was born. I want EntreLeaders who can be

- Passionately serving
- Mavericks who have integrity
- Disciplined risk takers
- Courageous while humble
- Motivated visionaries
- Driven while loyal
- Influential learners

Are you getting the idea? We wanted the personal power of the entrepreneur polished and grown by a desire to be a quality leader. We wanted big leaders who have the passion and push of the entrepreneur. These character qualities are what we look for in potential leaders and what we intentionally build into our team every day to cause us to win.[62]

This has become more of a common idea over the last ten years. All kinds of books have popped up about corporate entrepreneurship and "intrapreneurial leaders." I hope, as a creative, you share some of this mindset. Since we love to create, I believe this is part of our DNA—this entrepreneurial bent.

So why do I bring this up in a chapter on finances? Just like an entrepreneur needs to focus on the right things to grow the company, a creative leader needs to do the same thing.

Verne Harnish is known as "the growth guru" for small business owners. As a new leader, I want you to think about your area as a small business—an area that you need to grow. To do that you need to be sure to focus on the right financial things. Verne has a model he shares in his book, *Mastering the Rockefeller Habits: What You Must Do to Increase the Value of Your Fast-Growth Firm*. In his model there are three areas you need to satisfy: Customers, Employees, Shareholders. [63] Keeping these three areas in mind will put you in the right direction. How do you *stay* headed in the right direction? You need to ask yourself these questions:

- Do we have the right processes in place?
- Do we have the discipline for maintaining a competitive advantage?
- Is our organization/department/team structured properly?
- Can we deliver consistently?

As you grow over time, the answers to these questions will change. To maintain a profitable focus, Verne created a strategic framework that includes: [64]

1. Creating daily accountability
2. Reviewing a weekly schedule
3. Setting quarterly actions
4. Having annual goals
5. Envisioning three to five year targets
6. Following a purpose
7. Being guided by core values

Does any of this ring familiar? Focusing on the right things will propel you toward leadership success, financial success, and future success as well.

Before we close out this chapter, there is one last action I recommend. Make a habit of reviewing and aligning your products, projects, and processes.

Aligning Your Portfolio of Products, Projects, and Processes

Michael Watkins, of the Harvard Business School and author of *The First 90 Days: Critical Success Strategies for New Leaders at All Levels*, shares an exercise for diagnosing your range of products, projects, and processes so you can plan and align for best results. Michael introduces the STARS model as a chief way to accomplish this: [65]

STARS Model

Start-up - you are charged with getting a new product or project off the ground.

Turnaround - you take on a floundering group, product, or project in order to get it back on track.

Realignment - you are to help and refresh a product or process that has drifted into trouble.

Sustaining Success - you are responsible for not only sustaining but elevating products and processes to the next level.

Take time to review and list your products—their health, vision, and direction. Next, list all the projects you and your team have regarding these products. List the scope, timelines, and team resources for each project. Finally, list and review your team and project processes—are they in line with the pace and quality you are expected to demonstrate?

Now, take time to assign each of these to one of the four categories in the grid below. You may want to make a grid for each category: products, projects, processes. You can also color code them in the grid so you can quickly see and align what areas are out of balance. Afterward, consider how you plan to lead and budget for each of these quadrants.

Start-up	Turnaround
Realignment	Sustaining Success

The world of *Administrivia* is filled with many impediments that can be challenging for a new creative leader. Set aside time to learn. In addition, learning and sharing business realities can provide a sense of ownership and entrepreneurial spirit with the team. I hope this chapter made administrative work easier to grasp, giving you a measure of confidence as you move forward.

Chapter 32

The Power Principle

He did not see himself as powerful or as a leader. His love was technology. After high school he attended the seventh oldest educational institution in the U.S.—Brown University. He was about to ride the wave with a computer science degree in 1982, two years before the transformational "1984" debut of the Macintosh personal computer. While completing his PhD, he had the good fortune of being employed at Adobe Systems and Xerox Palo Alto Research Center. Computing and digital technologies were soaring high, yet he realized that his passion was teaching the next generation of technologists.

He taught and consulted for the remainder of his career. Google, Disney, and Electronic Arts were a few companies that benefited from his research and expertise. However, in September 2006, a diagnosis of pancreatic cancer refocused his attention. As a professor, he felt he had limited influence over his students, but in his *last lecture* he would understand the power principle.

Power Is Temporary

Ever heard the phrase, "We are living on borrowed time"? For those of us in positions of power and authority, a variation holds true: We're living with temporary power. This is why I want to discuss what I call The Power Principle.

I was reminded of this the other day by my friend, Andy. He said that we're all given a certain degree of power. We all have influence in certain arenas of our lives—for a time. The power will not always last, and it *can* be taken away. He went on to say, "Have you ever noticed how there are some, that when their power is threatened, get all puffed up and try to use their power in order to increase or keep the power and influence they have?" This is immediately evident in dictatorships. When a dictator's power is threatened (either real or perceived), they immediately set about beating down—sometimes literally—through intimidation or removing the threat. They cannot stand the thought of losing power and will do almost anything to maintain a sense of control. The reality is all power is lost over time. Look at all the great cultures, leaders, governments, and countries throughout history. They thought they would last forever, but it was only borrowed time. That is why we need to recognize our "power" is temporary, and the best we can do is pass it on to the next generation.

Personal Power

What do you do when you recognize that you are the powerful person in an arena of life? Do you use your power constructively, or do you abuse your power, just because you can? Are you leveraging your power for the good of others or for your own selfish ambitions? How you use the power you have is tantamount to your legacy as a leader and the legacy of the culture you create.

The allure of personal power is subtle. "But I worked hard to get here. I deserve it!" are the heinous thoughts of entitlement. Be careful where that kind of thinking can lead. Andy made some good observations about those lurid areas that we may fall into and attempt to exert control and power:

- Bosses over employees
- Husbands over wives
- Fathers over children
- Wives over husbands
- Mothers over children

- Presidents over countries
- Firstborn over second-born children
- Coaches over players
- Teachers over students
- Pastors and priests over parishioners
- Police over civilians

How do you want to be remembered by your staff, your peers, your family, your neighbors? It is not too late to right past wrongs. Everyone has a story to tell about their lives and how they grew up. Don't let a bad past define your future.

What story do you want to tell? If you do not deal with it, the past will catch up to you eventually. Read about comedian, actor, and author Bill Cosby. Realize you have power to do good, and do not throw it away. Read about actor Mel Gibson or golfer Tiger Woods. All good things must come to an end, and it is the same for all great leaders. Read about Winston Churchill, Ghandi, or Mother Teresa.

Your Last Lecture

On September 18, 2007, (if you have not guessed it from the opening story) professor Randy Pausch delivered *his* last lecture entitled "Really Achieving Your Childhood Dreams." This lecture gained notoriety as it was released on the web. Later, Disney-owned Hyperion Books published "The Last Lecture" that some of you may have read, and many will have heard about. The book became a *New York Times* bestseller in 2008 and has since been translated into 46 languages.

Randy did not see himself as powerful nor as a leader, but he poured out what he had for the benefit of others. This side of eternity he never had any idea of all the lives he would touch and influence by his last lecture.

The far-sighted person will understand that the power he has is only temporary. Eventually, those of us in power will lose it. As a matter of record, power can be taken away in the blink of an eye. Look at past and recent news about business scandals, church scandals, and national scandals. Power is not something to be held onto—it is something to be given away.

Are you convinced?

So the overarching question is: What are you doing with the power you have for the time you have it? Only a very secure leader is willing to give power away (see chapter twelve on Leadership Insecurity). I encourage you to give your power away—daily. Use your power to better your team, your department, and your organization.

Chapter 33
Replace Yourself

You may be thinking, "What do you mean 'replace yourself'? I just got here!" The title of this chapter runs against the grain of many who are new to leadership. Yet, my friend Dennis took this to heart throughout his career, and he is glad he did. To learn why, keep reading.

While it was later in his career that Dennis first heard about replacing himself as a leader, he had an inkling of the concept after moving to Albuquerque, New Mexico, to build a team for a radio station. What started as a concept came into sharper focus as Dennis led a larger radio station in Tulsa, Oklahoma, and then Los Angeles, California. Yet, it all made sense later when he became part owner and CEO of the leadership training company, Maximum Impact. You see, a question that had begun burning in his mind had now become fully formed. This is a question he asks all his leaders: What kind of legacy are you leaving?

When asked about this idea, Dennis' initial thoughts turned to his father, who led a church for many years. Dennis' father took the time to stay and build an organization opposed to the typical model of the period— building up a team over a short time then moving on to the next opportunity to build up a team and so on. This serving and investing leadership style was modeled early for Dennis. His definition of success was distinctly different from other leaders. "Were you truly a success or just a success in your own eyes?" Dennis asks leaders who move onto other roles or other organizations. "Are you building your own career path where it is all about 'you' or, when you leave a position, is the organization better than when you came?" More importantly, are those you lead better leaders having seen the leadership you model?

His first recollection of practicing this principle was with an employee named Jerry. Dennis saw potential in Jerry. He gave Jerry more responsibility as he proved himself faithful over time. There were chances given to try and fail and try and succeed. "My role," Dennis says, "was to provided guardrails." Over time, Dennis mentored and groomed Jerry. When Dennis left the company, Jerry was announced as his successor. Now, thirty-five years later, Dennis is still connected with Jerry as well as many of his former employees —most of which have very successful careers.

Dennis also told me, "If you see and treat each team member as a 10, they will strive to meet that bar." Be their biggest cheerleader no matter what part they play on the team. Good advice.

In 2006, the day finally came to leave Maximum Impact. Dennis knew it was time to move into another season of life, so he called a meeting of the entire staff. He handed the reins to a team of leaders who were more than capable of carrying on his leadership legacy. During his farewell meeting, he was presented with a journal. The journal was full of notes from employees apprising Dennis of what he had meant to them and how he had helped and inspired them to grow. He left a legacy of impacted lives.

As Dennis looks back he thinks, "A good leader is one whose legacy is carried on. One who has prepared those around him or her. You are always building a team and a legacy. There is nothing more rewarding than to see people move on to bigger and better things." While the businesses and organizations have grown and changed, the people and the lives of his team members who were influenced and impacted have been his greatest reward. Many of the life lessons Dennis learned as a leader he captured in his book called, *The Rancher's Gift*.

As Dennis and I spoke, I asked him what he would say to a new creative leader. Dennis' words to you are:

"Live on purpose; prepare for your exit; impart what you have learned to those around you—don't just take it for granted. Build relationships with the team and still be their leader. You cannot be their best friend, but they need to know you care. Their success is your success. Know what is important to them.

"The hiring process it crucial. Learn better skills in hiring—better questions. Look for people that are goal oriented, who place greater importance on the customer and fellow team members than themselves. Then, if you hire wrong, and you will, then the greatest gift you can give them is to release them. For me, it's not about the plaques on the wall, or the accolades, but it's the people—living breathing lives that are important. For me it's always about a leader's legacy—a legacy that does not stop beyond this generation."

Reputation

While talking with Dennis, several principles came to mind that I often share with my children, mentees, and leaders. Did you know that you have a reputation? When people think of you, they believe something about you. Those beliefs can run the gamut. People could believe you to be a hard worker or a procrastinator, trustworthy or deceptive, a promise keeper or promise breaker. Every day you are either adding to, building, or tearing down your reputation.

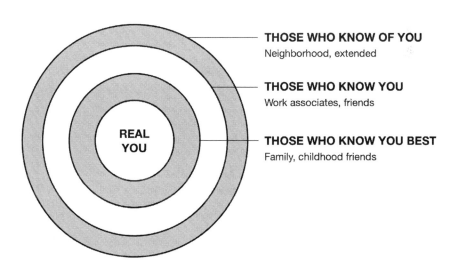

THOSE WHO KNOW OF YOU
Neighborhood, extended

THOSE WHO KNOW YOU
Work associates, friends

THOSE WHO KNOW YOU BEST
Family, childhood friends

REAL YOU

Adding to Your Reputation

Within your relational sphere you have a reputation. Some outside of your sphere may even have heard about you from co-workers and/or family and friends. Whether you have a positive or negative reputation, you are confirming what others already feel about you. Your reputation can be fluid. You may have one reputation at work and another one in your neighborhood. I hope your reputation is solid and consistent because it only takes one incident for it to come crashing down. This begs the questions: What is your reputation built upon?

Building On Your Reputation

At this point in your life you have built a foundation on how you act and treat people. Building on your reputation foundation happens in the here and now. As a new leader, you may be building a reputation with peers and the team, but you are building on an established foundation. Ask yourself (and others) what is your reputation built on? If that foundation is positive, I hope you continue to build a skyscraper that people will see and admire. This idea applies to team members as well. Help employees build a good reputation. Find means to increase their visibility. Help senior leaders become exposed to the team's top talent.

If your reputation is negative, you should tear it down. Excavate the bad habits and mental patterns. Begin to build a newer and better reputation foundation today.

Tearing Down Your Reputation

Tearing down a reputation, and breaking up the foundation takes time and effort. This can be done either in a positive or negative fashion.

Positively - You have done a lot of introspection and soul-searching. You have talked to family, friends, and co-workers who know you well. While you did not always like what they had to say, the evidence was conclusive—you have some work to do. You have some junk to rid yourself of, and it is okay. You have known there were issues, and now you are ready to deal with them constructively.

Negatively - You have been headed down a dark path. You have talked to family, friends, and co-workers who know you well. You did not like what they had to say and, frankly, it is not your fault—no matter what the evidence says. Your reputation has been solid until now. You feel shaken. You are hurt and mad. You have some junk, but doesn't everybody? You do not see the need to do anything, while others watch you spiral down destructively.

A reputation impacts your present. What people think about you *now*. Reputation can be changed. If you truly want to know how, talk to those around you. Ask them what they see that you need to change. It is not too late. On the other hand, a legacy is more permanent.

Leaving a Legacy

I have been training leaders since 1999—some of it professionally and much of it as a volunteer and mentor. Over the last few years one of the exercises I ask leaders to do is write their eulogy.[66] I know it sounds morbid at first, but all agree it is one of the most insightful, provocative, and meaningful exercises they do. As a group, we take turns reading our eulogies out loud. Hearing these leaders read what they want to have said about them gives each a worthwhile target to aim at for the future.

Your legacy is more everlasting and cannot be changed. You have moved on—either to another place of employment or to the afterlife. While reputation can be changed and is current, legacy is how you will be remembered. This leads me to a few questions: What do you aspire to *now*? How do you want to be remembered when you are gone?

Dennis' Final Comments

In closing out this section, Dennis had a few parting words. "It's incredibly important to read books to get a clear understanding about leadership. Read about great leaders you want to follow, but to *be a great leader* it has to start with you," he said. "Don't expect your team to follow you without first and always working on yourself. It is important to understand, read, and have leadership modeled by those you respect, but the bottom line is—it begins with *you*."

It is not always easy to be a leader. As a creative leader, you see the world a little bit differently. You approach challenges from a fresh perspective. However, as humans we all make mistakes. As humans, sometimes we know what to do yet do the opposite. Push against that. Find creative ways to be generous with your time and influence. Give yourself to the team—it is an investment in your future as well as theirs.

Applications for Week 10

This week you learned accounting basics, being generous with your time and influence, and that giving back to the team not only impacts your reputation but creates a legacy for your future.

Practical Applications

This week has only two applications:

1. Career development research
2. Write your eulogy.

Career Development Research

Think about the next step in your career. Picture it in your mind's eye where you want to be in two to three years. What do you see? How will you get there? Create a list of the things you need to pursue and accomplish to make that next career step a reality. Items might include:

- Researching company career paths to see what is available
- Conferences and webinars that would be appropriate to where you want to move
- Mentoring with a senior leader for exposure and networking
- Temporary Work Assignments (TWAs) to learn and get exposure

Now, think about the team members. You have met with them one-on-one. You have created a Team Profile Sheet (TPS) for each member. You asked each team member to begin a Career Development Plan (CDP). How can you help them aspire to *their* career goals? Review each TPS and list the actions you recommend each team member accomplish to make their next career step real. Before the next one-on-one, ask the employee to bring their finished CDP with them to the meeting. Review your TPS list and the CDP with each employee. Get their feedback, make revisions, and encourage them to finalize goals to achieve their desired career. Items might include:

- Researching career paths
- Conferences and webinars
- Mentoring with a manager
- Temporary Work Assignments to learn and get exposure
- Career Development Plan (CDP) outlining goals, action plans, strengths and future skills to develop

Check with your Human Resources department to see what resources are available to you for career development. Some of these resources you may be aware of since attaining your new role. Some you may not have had exposure to yet. Your Human Resources connection is your ally. If you do not have an HR department, seek out other leaders in your area for advice and recommendations.

Write Your Eulogy

As you think about your legacy, what do you want to be remembered for? This exercise is designed to provide a target for you to aim for in your life *and* career. You will create a eulogy from the viewpoint of a family member or friend talking about you at your farewell party or funeral. Use your creativity while touching on the following points:

- Write for your audience - who do you see attending this event?
- Include a brief life history.
- Be funny and somber.
- Provide some details about family.
- Touch on work, interests, and hobbies.
- Write it out verbatim.
- Close with inspirational words, something you would say, or a song/poem.
- Write no more than one page, front and back.

When you have completed your eulogy, put it someplace you will remember and set a calendar reminder to reread it a year from now. This will be a good opportunity to ask yourself if you are becoming the person you want to become.

I Answered That Question

This week we will focus more intently on the team/department culture you want to create. A culture of ownership, integrity, mutual trust, and responsibility. This is what will propel you and your team forward. Other employees will hear about and be attracted to this kind of team, and be envious of the work environment you have created.

- Create Culture and Reinforce
- What Do You Think?
- Treat People Like Adults
- Week 11 Practical Applications

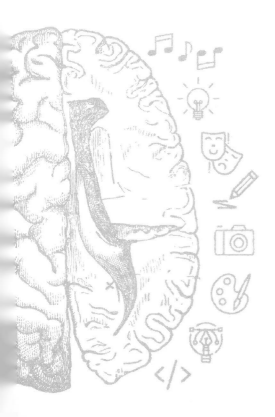

Chapter 34

Create Culture and Reinforce

culture

noun

civilization, society, way of life, lifestyle; customs, traditions, heritage, habits, ways, mores, values.

I was consuming a lot of books on leadership. I was painfully aware of my own inadequacies as it related to management. I also knew the kinds of leadership styles I had been exposed to—those I liked and those I abhorred. For me, I had found that I was the most productive when I was having fun (more to come on this), when I was working out of my strengths, when I believed in what I was working on, and when those around me were having fun, working out of their strengths, and believing as well.

I searched out other leaders in the organization that wanted to learn and grow. We started meeting for weekly breakfasts and sharing practical ideas. We started reading books together and wrestled over the principles and business theories espoused within. We put into practice what we learned.

I had daily stand-ups with my direct reports (before Agile was a thing), weekly department meetings, and brainstorm sessions. I included subject matter experts (SMEs) from other departments and even my own administrative assistant (who would say she was not creative) to add new and diverse perspectives.

One day I was approached by a leader from another department.

"Eric, I am working on my MBA and have to write a paper on leadership development. I have seen what you've been doing with your departments and wondered if I could interview you for my paper?"

"Of course, I'd be happy to help," I said.

Over subsequent weeks we met, and I answered all her questions about what I was doing, how I was doing it, and why I was doing it. She finished her paper and allowed me to read it. I thought her conclusions were fair and balanced.

She and several other leaders from around the company had heard, not from me but from my team, about the culture that *we* had created. They were passionate and excited about the work and the people they worked with. This enthusiasm spread so that others wanted to work in our area. That is the weight of culture.

Culture is a powerful thing. All companies have it. Departments have it. Even teams have a unique culture. The question becomes, "Is each culture the same or different?" —and—"Does it matter if they are?"

My friend, Dr. Tim Elmore, made some interesting observations. He studied world events and how each generation since the 1950s has viewed leadership. He recognized how leadership styles have evolved over the years. He then categorized a series of leadership styles based upon his findings. The brief descriptions below were taken from his white paper: *A New Kind of Leader.*[67]

The Military Commander — (1950s–1960s Generation)

This leader's organizations are run in a top-down fashion. Leaders lead and followers follow. Period. Employees don't question authority. If someone leaves a staff position, they are considered disloyal. These leaders enjoy leading from their positional authority.

The CEO — (Late 1960s–1970s Generation)

This leader leads by casting vision, in hopes that their followers will buy in and work toward fulfilling the vision. Productivity is the buzzword.

While this style is an improvement over the one above, it is still very top-down in nature.

The Entrepreneur — (Late 1970's–1980's Generation)

This leader is pioneering and doesn't do things the conventional way. They manage "by walking around." They feel the most critical element is being the *first* to do it. Innovation is a revered quality. This style enables employees to share ideas that might be implemented and helps them tolerate the fact that the leadership is still a top-down model.

The Coach — (1990s Generation)

This style is appealing to Gen-Xer's, who long for relationships and authenticity. This leader assembles and works with teams. They see themselves as coaches who have players. The leader finds the proper roles for all the players, so they can make significant contributions to the team. Although this style is participatory, it is still top-down in nature.

The Poet/Gardener — (2000's–Today's Generation)

This leader combines many of the strengths of the last four styles. Tim calls these leaders *poets* because they are discerning of the culture and the ideas that emerge from others, not just themselves. They synthesize and extrapolate thoughts, then they come up with the best one, even if it's not their own. These leaders are attractive to a new workforce who longs to be part of creating the ideas and determining the direction. This leader sees his primary function as *gardening*—developing his people. Tim says, "They are equippers. They empower.... [Employees] are not *used* by their boss—they are developed." This leader values growth—not just organizationally but for each individual in it. They lead out of shared ownership.

Tim goes on to say, "I believe [the poet/gardener] is the attractive leader of today. This isn't to say all the others will die out. Based on temperament and generation, other styles will remain, and some will do well, because of the strength of the leader's personality and vision. But the style that the new generation of employees will want is the poet/gardener."

I agree.

Shared Ownership and Culture

I want to talk a little more about this idea of shared ownership as it relates to the kind of culture you will be creating. *Ownership* is defined as the act, state, or right of possessing something. And while you and your team may not possess the company, they are in fact part owners. Their work, ideas, and the experience they bring to the organization impact the health, care, and well-being of the organization. When the organization succeeds, the employee succeeds and vice versa.

Impress upon your team that the work they do is important, not just to the customer and company, but to them as well. Be willing to share financials with your team. Help your team understand the impact they are making on customers and to the bottom line.

Jack Stack has a regular huddle with his organization and shares the numbers. He wants his employees to have "skin in the game." As CEO, you would expect him to look at the numbers regularly, but as an "open book" company, he shares financials openly. This has created a unique culture for his company—one of shared ownership. Jack, in his book *The Great Game of Business*, says it like this:

> It doesn't bother me to see that we have problems. The important thing is whether or not people are working toward solutions. We're always going to have problems. The question is, what are we doing to fix the problems? The numbers give me perspective. They tell me what's really important and what isn't important.
>
> The numbers also provide me with the security I need to let people take risks. They show me how far I can let people go before I have to step in and pull them back. That's very important. If you want people to grow, you have to let them take risks, and you have to let them fail. The tricky part is knowing how much to let people fail, where to draw the line. The numbers are my guide. They tell me when one person's failure, or one department's failure, is endangering others. [68]

The numbers not only help him make decisions, but they also help his people stay informed in how they make decisions. I am not saying you need an "open book" team or department. You will need to talk to your HR and finance departments about that. I am saying create a sense of ownership and accountability that gives team members something to care about and desire to work toward other than a paycheck.

Are you feeling any concern or tension about these ideas? Do you feel like you do not have access to the information? I had a former manager who took the time to find out the numbers and trends within the organization and started doing a bi-annual share-out with the team. His share-out became so popular that word got around, and he began sharing with multiple departments. After his presentation, we all knew where we stood financially, where the trends were headed, and how we impacted the bottom line. It was not only informative, but it was empowering too.

Integrity and Culture

Creating a positive and energetic culture can be reinforced by maintaining a high standard of integrity. Integrity is defined as having honesty and strong moral principles; a state of being whole and undivided. One way I have heard integrity defined is this: *Integrity is who you are when no one is watching.* I like that definition. The fact is we all do better when someone is watching, but what about when no one is? Are you consistent with your words and actions? Are your people consistent—whole and undivided?

I want to encourage you to make this one of the cornerstones of the culture you create. This is not easy and only comes over time with a lot of effort. It first begins with you. Seek out a close friend, a trusted peer, or a spouse and ask them to hold you accountable to integrity. Ask them to help you practice integrity. What? Yes, practice integrity. What you practice you *will* become.

Next, require integrity of the team. While you certainly want to give them the benefit of the doubt in most issues, you also want to watch them and see if they are exhibiting the integrity and culture you are trying to create. Are they trustworthy? Have they been able to accomplish the tasks and projects you have given them? Dave Ramsey says in his book *EntreLeadership,* you should look for integrity and competency:[69]

> Don't think because you hired talent that they are competent. Competency is more than just the simple ability to accomplish the task. Competency involves how the task was accomplished. How did all the people involved feel? Were all the problems handled right? Were all the downsides considered? Were the financial considerations of cash flow and profit accounted for and handled?

As team members earn trust, you allow more responsibility. As they prove themselves, you allow more until you hardly have to check on them. Remember, you are not micromanaging here; you are trying to create a sustainable, fun, high-performance culture. You want to make sure people are practicing, understanding, and fitting in appropriately.

Leadership and Culture

As you can see, as goes the leader goes the culture. What kind of leader are you?

The culture you create is of huge importance. No matter what kind of culture you have come from or experienced in your past, you need to create a healthy and vibrant one for your team.

Think back on the leaders you have admired. The leaders of whom you thought, "If I become a leader one day, I want to be like them." I hope the leader you had in mind was one who put their employees and customers first. Without engaged employees, you have no growing business. Without engaged customers you have no business—period.

Make culture key.

Chapter 35
What Do You Think?

"Boss, I have a problem…"

These are words you will likely hear from someone on your team. Other variations you may hear are:

What do you think I should do…?

Who do you think I should talk to…?

Where do you think I should go…?

When do you think I can…?

How do you think this should…?

These kinds of questions are not uncommon to leaders new and seasoned. You have employees that are either new to the working world, new to your company, new to your team, or new working with you as a leader. They may not yet understand the cultural norms or the connections they need to make to get their job done.

While you certainly want a team that will collaborate, and you don't want any Lone Rangers, you do want people that are responsive and proactive. You want top-notch A-players who can thrive in a collaborative team environment and also get the work done.

Yet, sometimes you will find yourself in what can almost be described as a parental role. Here you will need to exercise balance. Don't spoon-feed employees, but help them think for themselves. Show them you trust and value their insights.

One of the best pieces of advice I got from another leader on this topic was to turn the tables and ask the employee, "That's a good question. What do you think?"[70] This is Coaching 101—help people help themselves. You cannot answer every question or afford to take on many of their issues. Help the employee form a plan and hold them accountable to seeing it through.

Trust Funnel

The image below illustrates how trust and responsibility can grow over time. Early in the relationship there is low trust because, frankly, you do not know the person that well. As you get to know them, coach them, mentor them, and work with them over time, you can give more responsibility. As they prove faithful with an effort, trust grows. Notice, however, that when trust is broken, the process often has to start all over again. Depending on the significance of the infraction, you may question whether you really knew the person to begin with. Be wary of giving too much trust too soon. Trust has to be earned *consistently over time*. We see this apply in many other areas of life, and we should apply it in business as well.

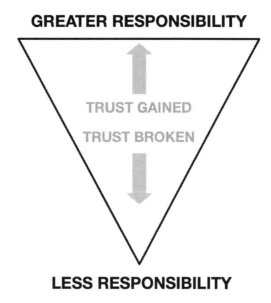

GREATER RESPONSIBILITY

TRUST GAINED

TRUST BROKEN

LESS RESPONSIBILITY

You Are Not Alone

The late Stephen R. Covey had an interesting interview with Frances Hesselbein, CEO of the Frances Hesselbein Leadership Institute (formerly the Leader to Leader Institute) and editor in chief of the *Leader to Leader* journal.[71] During the interview, Covey hit on the common issue of a company culture moving from control to commitment:[72]

> **FH:** You have hit on a major issue that leaders face: moving from a culture of control—old hierarchy—to a culture of commitment and inclusion and alignment. How do we do it? Would we look at mission? Would we look within ourselves? What is the first step?
>
> **SRC:** I think the first step is deep reflection on what your own life is about. What are your values? Do you have a bone-deep belief in the potential of other people, and do you truly want to see that potential identified and released and recognized? Otherwise, you may talk a good game, but you are just using a new, more subtle form of control.
>
> In an opportunity to interview leaders...I asked each, "What was the toughest struggle you had?" To a person they all said, giving up control. They all feared the consequences of letting go. But ultimately, they found their fears were groundless— they found an unimagined resource capability that emerged when there was common vision and a common value system.
>
> **FH:** Stephen, are you saying that these leaders simply made a leap of faith to give up control and unleash the energy of the organization? Or was there some spadework they had to do before taking that step?
>
> **SRC:** There was some spadework. These leaders sought the participation of people throughout their organization and beyond. But it was an almost daily question of, "Wow, do we really want people that involved? Do we want them that informed? Do we want them to have that much freedom of

action?" These executives struggled constantly, in a very personal way, to let go, step back, and change their role.

Seeking input and affirmation from "the boss" is not a new thing. But being the person with all the answers does not help your team members grow nor does it communicate interest in their thoughts and ideas. Do not handicap your staff by having to always give permission. Allow for failure and risk. As John Maxwell says, "fail forward."

Weeding and Planting

Remember the temperament types we discussed at the beginning? Be cognizant of the differing temperaments that may consistently pander to you asking for your input or approval. This could be due to a previous leader they worked with or an unhealthy culture they came from. I have found these types fall into three camps. I call them the CYAers, the Pleasers, and the Schmoozers.

The CYAer

The Cover-Your-A$$er (CYAer) is *afraid of making a mistake* and the fallout that can come from overbearing bosses or micromanagers. They will always ask what you want and what you think they should do and how to do it. I hope you have not created a culture that supports those individuals.

Let this person know they do not need to be afraid of making an honest mistake. The cultural seed you want to plant is to *learn* from mistakes, *share* their learnings, and help the team keep moving forward.

The Pleaser

The Pleaser lives in fear. They *want to please those around them*. They may be hard workers and very diligent, yet there's an unhealthy undercurrent rooted in wrong motivation—pleasing those around them to gain acceptance. They will go to great lengths to do this. While you are not called upon to solve your employee's personal problems, you should understand this kind of personality will have issues making hard decisions because of their overarching need to please. They will have a hard time standing up for their ideas, even when they are right.

The cultural seed you want to plant is that *diversity of thoughts and ideas* are a good thing. The only bad idea is the one that goes unvoiced. Encourage open debate during meetings and let this person know that you need their unfiltered participation. Help them understand that if their idea is not picked, it does not devalue them as a person. The team should agree and commit to the best ideas no matter whom they come from.

The Schmoozer

Finally, the Schmoozer is *out for themselves*. They are motivated by selfish advancement. Like the CYAer, they will often ask what you want and what you think they should do and how to do it. They do this to be perceived as a team player. Don't be mistaken—they are typically out for themselves.

The Schmoozer is the most difficult type to work with. They feel they can trust no one but themselves. It could be they have been disappointed by others over the course of their lifetime. They may feel the only person they can rely on is themselves. They want to control and influence and have learned that aligning themselves with influencers gives them an ego boost.

The cultural seed you want to plant with this person is *accountability*. You want this person to know the kind of team culture you are trying to build and that there is no favoritism. You will temper this by helping them understand your desire to see them grow and succeed.

So, the next time a member of your team comes up to you asking for your opinion, ideas, or how to get a project done, listen to them and then ask, "What do *you* think?"

Chapter 36
Treat People Like Adults

Fred.

"It's not my fault. My wife has had to travel, and my kid has been sick. I've needed to come in late and take extra time away," Fred said. "I am doing my best to stay on top of the work, but sometimes I have to chauffeur my kid to the doctor."

"These things happen, Fred. I understand that. Yet now, the team expectation is that you won't be here and we're having to shift work around to make sure projects get covered."

Stacie.

"I have a doctor appointment I totally forgot about. I will be out for the latter half of today," Stacie said. "I am really sorry. It is my fault. I had this on my calendar and forgot to put it on the company calendar. This is so unlike me. I reached out to Jean about covering for me while I was away, so we are all good for today. I will make up the time over the next fews days if that's okay?"

"Thanks, Stacie, for letting me know and taking care of this. I appreciate you finding Jean to fill in for you while you're out. You know what you need to do to stay on top of the work. I do not expect you to put in extra hours unless you feel you need to."

Contrast Stacie's situation with Fred's. Stacie was apologetic and took responsibility while Fred seemed a victim of his circumstances. Stacie was proactive in finding someone to help fill in while she was away whereas the manager had to shift work around in order to cover for Fred. This seemed a rare situation with Stacie while with Fred, the team expected his behavior.

While these situations are all too real, and the circumstances may not entirely be an employee's fault, the impact to the team and the work is affected. As an adult, people like Fred should and can find a way to mitigate situations. A candid call with his manager, taking an extended leave of absence, or just working with his peers and teammates to cover for the work that needs to be done are all solutions Fred could have pursued. The goal is to make circumstances like this an anomaly and not the norm.

Cultural Norms

As you create or establish norms within the team culture, you are setting standards, expectations, and behavioral guidelines they should follow. Consider long and hard the cultural norms you want to create. Below is a list of several norms to aspire to and reinforce.

Helpful Not Helpless

Why does it seem like many adults have "learned helplessness?" Why have we as leaders and managers let so many employees get away with sloppy sub-par work and attendance? Dave Ramsey calls this "sanctioned incompetence." [73]

Am I advocating for a hard-nosed leadership style? No way. Am I settling for a relaxed, nonchalant method of doing business? Nope. People want to be treated like adults even when they don't always act grown-up. Do not baby people, and do not put up with childish behavior. One of Dave's EntreLeadership principles speaks to this topic: [74]

> "Treat others as you want to be treated" is a core EntreLeadership principle. When you would expect to be praised, praise. When you would expect a raise, give a raise. When you would need training, train. When you would need some grace, give some grace. When you would expect a reprimand, give one. When you would feel competent and

want the dignity of being left to do the job, back off and let the competent execute.

Create a culture of helpful not helpless employees. Ask your team and peers regularly, "How can I help?" Do not offer it as a platitude, nor as a way to micromanage but offer to help where you can, as you can. The team will start to pick up on this attitude. As this norm takes root, you and your team will be highly thought of and respected.

Blameless Not Blameworthy

We do not live in a perfect world. Work can and will go sideways at times. Take ownership when you or the team are at fault—be apologetic. Even if it was a misunderstanding, be willing to "take the hit." Be humble. An apology costs you nothing, but it pays dividends with the team when they see appropriate humility. This is your role as a leader. Strive to be blameless in all you do and set that example for the team. Like Stacie, apologize for your mistakes—own up to them. Act like an adult and treat others the same way.

Responsible Not Irresponsible

Sometimes a person might be *the victim* of a predicament, but he or she is not *a victim*. There is a difference. The former recognizes he has choices and decisions he can make to assuage what is going on. The latter feels powerless and is carried on the current of helplessness. He is too absorbed with the situation to see a way out. His focus is on himself, which it should be for a time, but he needs to learn to unite with others. Be a person who shares and takes responsibility. Think of any great leaders through history who have risen above their circumstances. It almost always started with an *attitude* and then moved to an *action* which brings us to our next norm.

Proactive Not Inactive

Notice how Stacie reached out first and did not wait until after the appointment to say something. You want to be proactive, and you want that for the team as well. Depending on their temperament, some may find this norm outside their comfort zone. This may be you. Some creatives feel uncomfortable "putting themselves out there." Improving yourself and others often means putting yourself "out there."

- Reach out first.
- Set up the meeting first.
- Make the announcement first.
- Apologize first.
- Recognize and communicate the issue first.
- Start the conversation first.
- Talk to customers first.
- Correct mistakes first.

You will see confidence grow in yourself and others as you become more proactive.

Thriving Not Striving

Stacie was willing to put in extra hours to make up for the work that was missed. How do you get that kind of attitude from an employee? Some are naturally responsible people, but you *want* a culture like that. You want a team that is thriving, growing, learning, happy, innovative, and adapting well. All the weeks leading up to this have been building toward a culture worth being a part of—a culture to create.

A Culture Worth Creating

The cultural norms above are only a few examples of the standards and expectations you can set for the team. Think back over your career. What were the behaviors, attitudes, qualities and practices that inspired you to be and do your best? As we discussed earlier, who are the leaders you admire and why? Could it be the culture they had created was one that you would love to mimic?

Employees crave a consistent, fun, and healthy environment—one where they can use their strengths and thrive amongst peers who challenge them to be their best, a culture that appreciates them and treats them like adults. Is that not a culture worth coming to work for, a culture worth creating?

The applications for this week will assist you in the process of creating a culture you and the team will love. Like all the applications prior, please do not rush through the exercises. You are building a future that other leaders will admire and likely envy. It is worth the work.

Applications for Week 11

Don't create a fear of failure culture—fail fast, learn, and keep moving forward. Create the kind of culture you want to come to work for every day.

Practical Applications

This week there are two applications:

1. Leader List.
2. Pace and Quality worksheet.

Leader List

As we discussed this week, think of the leaders in your life that you aspire to become more like. What was it about them that inspired you? List the leader and top three qualities, values, or practices you desire to implement in your life and team culture. After you make your list, put together an action plan to change or implement this in your area.

LEADER NAME	Qualities	Values	Practices
ACTION PLAN			

Pace and Quality Worksheet

By now, you should have set up a regular cadence of one-on-one weekly meetings and a monthly team retrospective. At this point you are building momentum. Increasing pace and quality are key. Use the worksheet below to search for efficiencies and increase the pace of your work. This doesn't mean you want to sacrifice quality. Creative people can be pushed. They may find it frustrating at the beginning of a project but rewarding to see how much they were able to accomplish on the backend of the project. Be sure to give them encouragement and accolades for a job well done. This will contribute to team confidence and allow them to flourish.

Worksheet

EFFICIENCIES			
Work Process	Were processes followed: Y/N	If not, why not?	How can they be improved?
Collaboration	Was there significant collaboration?	If not, why not?	How can it be improved?
Communication	Was there effective communication?	If not, why not?	How can it be improved?
Operations	Are the tools adequate for the need?	If not, why not?	How can they be improved?

Methodologies	Is there a need for new or updated methodologies?	If not, why not?	How can they be improved?

PACE			
Deadline	Was the deadline met?	If not, why not?	How can it be improved?
Business Goal(s)	Were the business goals met?	If not, why not?	How can they be improved?
Objectives and Key Results (OKRs)	Were the OKRs clear?	If not, why not?	How can they be improved?
Stretch Goals	Were there stretch goals?	If not, why not?	How can they be implemented next time?
Additions/Creep	Were there last-minute additions or scope creep?	If so, why?	How can they be mitigated next time?

QUALITY			
Brand standards	Were the brand standards met?	If not, why not?	How can this be improved?

Accessibility standards	Were the accessibility standards met?	If not, why not?	How can this be improved?
Content standards	Were the content standards met?	If not, why not?	How can this be improved?
Media standards	Were the media standards met? (Print, web, video, etc.)	If not, why not?	How can this be improved?
Creative standards	Were the creative standards met?	If not, why not?	How can this be improved?
ACTION PLANS			

Feel free to apply these items to your area. If you are in food services, broadcast media creation, music—whatever your creative discipline, make these work for you.

You're So Creative

This week should feel like coming home. I wanted to end in familiar territory. Just because you are a new leader does not mean you stop being creative. On the contrary, you will need to be very creative and in new ways.

- Remote Work and Creativity
- The FUN Equation Equals Success
- Setting Aside Creative Time
- Week 12 Practical Applications

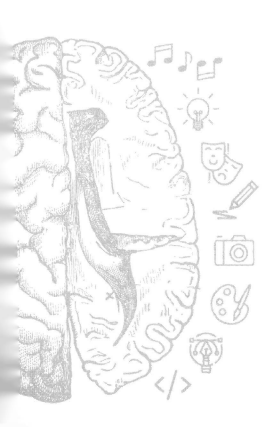

Chapter 37

Remote Work and Creativity

"What?! Work from home? Are you kidding me? I don't need you playing video games and watching TV when you should be here working."

"Oh yeah. Sorry about that. We were talking in the elevator yesterday morning and decided to take the project in a new direction. Yeah, you should probably video conference the creative director to make sure you're working on the right things."

"Sorry, you cannot work from home because everyone doesn't have that opportunity. It would not be fair to others if you worked from home while, because of their role, they aren't allowed."

"Productivity will take a dive. How are we going to brainstorm and whiteboard together?"

"We aren't set up to work remotely."

"We are not going to pay for you to set up a home office. What if your connection speed is too slow?"

"How can we effectively brainstorm remotely? It's not the same. We need to be together so we can bounce ideas off each other."

Do any of these statements sound familiar? When I first breached this subject of remote working years ago with my leadership, I heard similar responses. Now, we live in a new world. Today's digital workers and digital natives have changed where we work and how we work. Also, it took a pandemic in 2020 to throw out most of the statements above. Our economic, business, technical, and creative landscapes have changed considerably. It is amazing what we can do when we get creative and put our minds together for something like working remote.

Now, the challenges are no longer based on "can we or should we work remote." Many organizations struggle with efficiency- and culture-related issues when it comes to working remotely. Below are some tips and guidelines I have put together that begin to address these challenges. As for additional material, there are a myriad of online resources that you have at your fingertips. The recommendations here are based on working for three kinds of organizations over my career: an office environment, a virtual environment, and a hybrid environment. I believe the most applicable environment today will likely be the hybrid environment. While these guidelines are based on my personal experience and best practices, you should be creative in your approach to using them.

Efficiency and Remote Working

Pros

Productivity - contrary to historical points of view, working from home has increased productivity. Mercer, an HR and workplace consulting firm, conducted a recent study with 800 employers. [75] Ninety-four percent of these said productivity amongst remote employees was the same or better.

Early in - many remote workers are "at work" earlier because of no commute.

Focus time - because there are fewer interruptions from passing staff, remote workers feel they are more focused and get more work done as a result.

Flexibility - remote workers love the ability to start work early, run errands in the afternoon, and finish up later in the evening. Being able to flex with life's demands is very appealing.

Cons

Time zones - a challenge to working remote can be working across time zones. It is hard to take a break when your lunch time is during someone else's morning meeting. It may be dinner time on the East Coast while you have a counterpart who is still in the afternoon on the West Coast and expects you to be available.

Late out/never leaving work - another challenge with working remote is that you have, in essence, never left work. For some, this can lead to burnout as they work longer hours because the lines between work and home are blurred.

Focus with children/family dynamic - this is related to the challenge above. While focus on work may increase, focus on family and relationships can decrease. A remote worker needs to guard against this decline and so should you. (See chapter 22 on work-life balance.)

Multitasking - this can be challenging for remote workers as they may *feel* like they can answer email while listening to a meeting, or check text messages on mute while the rest of the team is collaborating. Multitasking is a myth unless you are performing a bodily function like eating.

No home office - for some, the lack of a place or space to convert into a home office can make remote working a challenge. While the local coffee shop promotes WiFi™, some workers prefer solitude and quiet in order to feel productive. It also promotes a professionalism others need to feel they are "at work."

Low bandwidth - while this can be overcome, some employees have never required higher speeds because of their digital usage. Now they are faced with the reality of video conferencing, and they may not be able to afford a monthly top-tier rate.

Tips for a Culture of Remote Working

Daily virtual stand-ups

Just as if you were in an office, having daily stand-up meetings remotely is a huge benefit. In a hybrid situation, this keeps Remote Joe and Jane in the loop if any hallway conversations happened without them. These meetings also hold everyone accountable.

Weekly collaboration meetings

Use available and approved audio/video tools for regular collaboration meetings. Sometimes, you may use multiple tools so you can screen share and whiteboard as well.

Open chat

I worked for a virtual company, and one of the best practices was keeping a company chat always open. Depending on the size of your organization, you might limit it to a department. It was the equivalent of the office break area or kitchen where you could grab someone at a moment's notice.

Remote etiquette - as remote working has become more prevalent, the need for establishing remote conduct and behaviors is essential. Here are some examples to build upon:

Video/dress - if you plan on using video regularly, you may desire a dress code. You don't want *Remote Joe* to enter a meeting looking disheveled while reporting to leadership.

Good mic or headset - avoid background noise and audio delay with a good mic and headset or earbuds. If you are not used to wearing a headset for most of the day, you will find your ears and head feeling sore. Investing in a comfortable set will spare you the irritation. It also helps with audio delay caused by using a computer's built-in microphone—that internal pause that alerts your mic that you are speaking.

Muting - learning to mute and unmute your mic is a must. If you are in a meeting and not talking, keep your mic muted. If you are in an "open" meeting room (like the open chat above but for audio), keep your mic muted unless you need to get someone's attention.

Animals/children - this one certainly depends on your situation and home office layout. If both Mom and Dad are working remotely and have multiple children, see if an older child can watch the younger ones. If both Mom and Dad are at the house and only one parent is working remotely, see if the other would be willing to watch any pets or children. If you are single with pets or children, a crate for the pet or sitter for the child are options. Older children can be taught that when Mom or Dad is "at work," they should not be disturbed unless there is an emergency.

Chatting - learning to think of your remote team can be difficult. If you are used to an office culture, you do not think anything about getting up to go to the restroom or break area. Your co-workers *see* you. However, working remote means you need to notify your team regularly. This may mean learning acronyms you are not used to using within chat.

If you plan to step away, let your team know you will *be right back* (brb) and send a note when you are back at your desk. If you need time to focus on work, let your team know you are "going heads down." Here are a few commonly-used acronyms you may not know, but be sure to talk to your co-workers ahead of time as these change frequently:

ICYMI: In case you missed it	IMO/IMHO: In my opinion/humble opinion
TL/DR: Too long, didn't read	IDK: I don't know
LMK: Let me know	TBA/TBD: To be announced/ determined

NVM/NM: Never mind	EOD/EOB: End of day/End of business
QOTD: Quote/Question of the day	NP: No problem
OOO: Out of office	N/A: Not applicable or not available
BRB: Be right back	TIA: Thanks in advance
TTYL: Talk to you later	CTA: Call to action
HMU: Hit me up	CTR: Click thru rate
FWIW: For what it's worth	+1: I agree
OTP: On the phone	AFK: Away from keyboard

Fatigue

Based on the team temperaments, watch out for remote worker weariness. Look for signs during one-on-one's or when in meetings. We humans were created for relationships (some more than others), and being or feeling isolated is not healthy.

Staying motivated

Looking at screens for long periods of time can cause eye strain, mental fatigue, and headaches. Taking frequent breaks throughout a day full of video meetings can help you stay alert and motivated. Look out a window to refocus your eyes. Minimize looking at mobile or tablet devices when off work. Move as much as you can, even during meetings. Turn off the video if you need to stand, or do deep knee bends to keep the blood flowing.

Office set up

Encourage the team members to set up an office space that is comfortable and efficient for the work they need to do. Understanding ergonomics and body dynamics is helpful when sitting for long periods of time. I have several friends who have made their own standing desks, giving them the option to sit and stand through the day. I also have friends who have modified their home treadmills so they can have a laptop available while they walk.

Setting expectations and creating culture

You have to be thinking about communications and collaboration with all parties involved. While you want flexibility, you may also request office hours to be during a consistent time so team members and vendors have access to each other. I know some organizations that request remote workers to be available between 10:00 a.m. and 3:00 p.m. Eastern Standard Time. The employee then chooses how to start and end their days in order to accomplish his or her required work. They now have some flex in their schedule to allow for home-related needs.

Efficiency and Remote Creativity

Pros

Smaller Budget - let's face it, you can keep the project overhead down when you have remote workers. You don't need to pay for or rent office space. And if you turn that into higher wages for the team members, you have a huge win-win.

No on-demand performing - creativity often comes when you least expect it. You know that. How many times have you left work only to have an epiphany about a project? It happens to me all the time. This is often your cognitive process going to work for you and pulling ideas together that you could not force while during "on-demand" work hours.

Focus - when the muse strikes, creatives love to focus on their projects. They can get an insane amount of work done. Granted, sometimes you just have to sit in your seat and gut-wrenchingly grind out the work, but when creatives are distraction free and can focus—look out!

Scheduling - creatives love flexibility in their work day. The ability to move around and get inspiration elsewhere is a big bonus.

Cons

Self-discipline - creatives can be notorious for lacking self-discipline. Heck, we all struggle with self-discipline. Creatives can get distracted in the creative process. One moment they are solving a design problem, and the next they are distracted by a text from their friend about *Leroy Jenkins*—how many of you are now searching for videos about Leroy Jenkins?

Collaboration - creatives like both solitude and collaboration to spark ideas. Collaboration in a remote environment can be especially demanding.

Coordination - depending on the kind of creative work you do, the coordination of efforts can be tough. For instance, a magazine designer may have a deadline for a printer proof. She is waiting on copy edits and revised photography before she can get the draft out the door. An audio engineer may be waiting for voice-over or musical talent to send in their files, but they were up late at a previous night's gig and have not finished their piece yet.

Project complexity - more and more creative projects are layered and more complex nowadays. Remote access to assets, project management, and timing are more grueling in a remote environment.

Tips for a Culture of Remote Creativity

Learning

Creatives tend to like diverse ideas and disciplines. Learning about new ideas, people, places, and things are part of a creative's DNA. Remote learning is more prominent than ever. Allow the team opportunities to continue learning and growing. It will add to their ideation catalog and add to your innovations.

Brainstorming

Tools abound for remote collaboration. Find what works for the team and the problem(s) you are trying to solve. Some brainstorm sessions can be synchronous while others can be asynchronous allowing members to think and ponder before they add to the brainstorm.

Weekly collaboration meetings

While remote, you want to promote regular collaboration among team members. The group size can vary, but having peers look at and speak into each other's work is incredibly beneficial.

Creative pauses

As noted above, creatives need a break from "work" to think about their projects. This can come in the form of a daily walk during lunch or going to a yoga class. Something to get the body moving and the blood flowing promotes ideation.

Side projects

Throughout my professional career, I have always had creative side projects going. They are often in another discipline or media as a way to keep the creative juices flowing and up-to-date. Allow the team members some other kinds of creative outlets to keep from getting stagnant.

Downtime

Like the creative pause, downtime is necessary. Creative work is hard and can be spontaneous. Encouraging regular time off is something you should do. It gives employees a chance to recharge. This can be hard for some, like me, because there is "always something to do." As a leader, you do not want to burn out folks—even the high performers. Talk to HR and see what policies you have in place or just tell a team member to take off half a day. You know who your employees are and who needs downtime.

Working remote is part of today's norm. How to be efficient and creative while doing so needs to be experimented with on a regular basis. Making sure the culture you are creating caters to remote work is a must.

I hope this chapter has sparked some new or fresh ideas that you can apply. Take what works and throw away the rest. Put your own spin on these tips and ideas. Above all, make it fun. We will learn more about that next.

Chapter 38

The Fun Equation

"This is so boring. I just want to learn to play the guitar."

"You *are* learning. You are learning the building blocks. These chords are what you need to learn to build upon. You cannot go straight to playing songs without learning proper fretting and chord structure."

I did not like guitar lessons in fifth grade. I wanted to play songs from Jimi Hendrix and Carlos Santana. Maybe I would try the piano instead. I liked Elton John. So my guitar sat in the corner for over thirty years gathering dust.

"You don't wanna play piano," a friend told me. "I have taken lessons for two years, and for the first year, all I did was practice scales."

"What's a scale?" I asked.

In eighth grade my musical interests grew. I listened to a wide variety of musicians and styles. The drums always looked fun. "Maybe I will try percussion," I thought to myself. After beating on my mother's Tupperware® for several months, I noticed a house in the neighborhood that had a handwritten sign in front reading "Private Drum Lessons - $20/hr" with a phone number to call. Of course, I called. The following week I showed up for my first drum lesson.

"So who do you like listening to?"

"Um, well...I like The Beatles, Boston, Led Zeppelin, Journey, and Rush," I said, "to name a few."

"Wow. What song are you listening to now?"

"'Don't Stop Believin' by Journey."

"Wanna learn to play that?"

"Yes!"

Arvin knew how to make learning and music enjoyable. Throughout the year that I took lessons from him, I learned the rudiments of drumming, but it was all in the context of songs I listened to and wanted to learn to play. By the time Arvin recommended a book for learning the basic rudiments, I was more than ready. I had built a foundation and desire to learn more as my skills had grown. All of this was due to Arvin. He provided me with information and the ability to apply it, but in the context of a fun environment where learning and work was exciting, refreshing, and gratifying.

Fun

Industries have been catching onto this idea of *fun* as a success catalyst more and more. For example, in a 2005 paper, Kurt Squire extolled the virtues of game-based learning: [76]

> ...games are much more powerful; they provide situated experiences in which players are immersed in complex, problem solving tasks. Good games teach players more than just facts; they provide ways of seeing and understanding problems and, critically, supply opportunities to "become" different kinds of people.

Let me make one thing clear, as noted in a previous chapter, I believe the idea of mandatory fun in the workplace is necessary. What I am not advocating is a top-down approach where fun is dictated, and everyone feels forced to take part. What I am advocating is that fun be part of the culture you create, where you and employees can generate ideas, play, and gamify work as a means to increase morale and enhance productivity. My idea of "mandatory fun" is where leadership values fun as a motivational factor in work and labors toward making it part of the culture. A more recent study came to this same conclusion. Ethan Mollick and Nancy Rothbard of the

University of Pennsylvania, The Wharton School Management Department, published a paper stating: [77]

> ...games that are imposed by management require worker consent in a way that games generated organically by workers do not. In our field experiment, we find that games, when consented to, increase positive affect at work, but, when consent is lacking, decrease positive affect.

A culture of imposed fun is not the goal. A culture where fun is valued and encouraged is the goal. This involves everyone and is endorsed by leadership—not as a means to get out of work, but as a way to generate positivity and consequently, innovative solutions that differentiate you from competitors.

Enter the Fun Factor

People ask me about my reference to the Fun Factor. This concept was something I posted on my blog back in 2007. The illustration below represents my philosophy for working, learning, teaching, communicating, and more. The Fun Factor applies to all generations.

As I have taught and mentored over the years, what I experienced as a child learning to play a musical instrument, I have seen others experience throughout life. Whether learning or working, while in school or in a career, being in a fun environment increases retention *and* elevates productivity. When retention is high, skills grow. When skills grow, you increase productivity and value—value for yourself and others.

A Physiological Perspective

Fun has a positive affect on you neurologically and physically. New, unusual, and surprising information is initially stored in your brains hippocampus. This part of the brain consolidates long-term memories and tries matching the new experience to existing patterns. When these patterns cannot be matched, there is a physical release of the chemical, dopamine. This chemical stimulates the amygdala, the emotional part of the brain, associating the new information with pleasant feelings.[78] What is the impact? New experiences under the umbrella of fun are retained in our long-term memory and associated with pleasurable emotions. What is the result? A desire for repetition.

As I contemplated this concept, I wondered how to express it best. What kind of expression is true no matter what? Mathematical expressions! 2 + 2 = 4 all the time, no matter the generation or culture. I thought of a mathematical equation as a way to capture this idea. If you do B and C multiplied by A you get X results. Here is how I describe it...

> We are consuming so much knowledge these days that, unless we apply what we learn, there is little to no retention or remembrance. What we apply, we have experiential knowledge of, and what we experience we like or dislike. As such, we can choose to make certain experiences part of our lives and discard others. This emotional response is most favorable when the entire process is multiplied by *Fun*.
>
> Applying knowledge in our lives within a fun environment has a positive response and, subsequently, repeats itself. This repetition creates a cycle that fosters *success* for both the person/organization transmitting and the person/organization receiving.
>
> **FUN x (KNOWLEDGE + APPLICATION) = RETENTION [the same as SUCCESS!]**

You can apply this equation, or recipe if you will, to most any endeavor and you'll find success. Let's look at it from a few more perspectives.

An Employee Perspective

As noted earlier, people enjoy fun experiences. What better way to raise morale than to incorporate fun into the workplace. The Fun equation builds on existing modes of learning and labor; information and experience. Take into consideration an employee's perspective.

Knowledge

The root word for *knowledge* comes from the Greek word *gnosis*, signifying knowing through observation or experience. Merriam-Webster's Dictionary defines knowledge as the "fact or condition of knowing something with familiarity gained through experience" and "the fact or condition of having information or of being learned."[79] Creatives by nature are learners and assimilators. Every experience adds to an internal library of ideas, concepts, shapes, and patterns. As a creative leader, encourage learning and training among the team. Look for opportunities to send people to conferences or workshops and start a team library.

Application

There is an old proverb that says, *wisdom is the application of knowledge*. A bias toward action is always better than passivity. Applying what you learn cements recent knowledge in your brain. It promotes additional learning and overcomes assumptions in lieu of real-world experience. As a creative leader, look for and encourage fun ways for the team to apply what they are learning.

Retention

This is a natural byproduct of applied knowledge. Repetition is one method to help retain knowledge. The more you apply a positive action, behavior, or knowledge the easier it is to retain. Other retention methods may include writing it down, drawing pictures, presenting the information, and teaching the information. Ask the team members which ways they best retain what they learn.

Productivity

With the retention of applied recent information comes productivity. New solutions. New ways of getting the work done. Positive feedback and other rewards encourage the employee to repeat the process. Remember, what gets rewarded get repeated. What is repeated is retained, and what is retained is knowledge applied within a culture of fun.

A Customer Perspective

Think of the businesses and events you frequent in person. As a customer, what is it that attracts you to these establishments—the ones that have become your favorites? The product is the more overt item people think of, but the culture and environment tend to be more covert, more sublime. We are subtly impressed by the energy, effort, and enthusiasm expressed by the people that work there. Take into consideration a customer or business partner's perspective as they interact with you.

Excitement

How did you hear about the last movie, restaurant, or event that you went to? It was likely word of mouth from a family member or friend. Why would they market a service or establishment from which they are not receiving compensation? Because they likely had a fun experience. There were probably a few surprises like a plot twist, unique flavors or activities that left a favorable impression. As a creative leader, look for ways to tangibly show excitement to your customers. Give them reasons to tell others about your business.

Refreshment

Many of us are familiar with the phrase "same old, same old." We use it for experiences that are the same, stale, and boring. What is it that makes something feel new and refreshing? There are typically two key moments in customer interaction where fun plays a key role: *entrance and exit*. As a creative leader, make that initial contact new, fresh, fun, and exciting. When a customer leaves, that interaction cements in their mind a memorable experience—one that felt personal and refreshing.

Gratification

Have you ever thought of an experience as gratifying? For what are you grateful? In this world we all have appetites. Appetites for adventure, love, fulfillment, meaning, and companionship. When these appetites are met, we feel a sense of gratification. We want to feel that again and again. As a creative leader, bringing fun into your culture can leave a customer feeling gratified for having interacted with you.

Thirty-some-odd-years later, I dusted off my old guitar. It was in need of restringing so I took it to the local music store. The employees could not believe how old the guitar was nor the great condition it was in. I laughed and told them it was because it had not been played in over thirty years.

"So why are you fixing it up now?" an employee asked.

My daughter started guitar lessons about a month before this encounter. For the first lesson, her instructor showed up at the house wearing a T-shirt from a recent *Boston* concert. I liked him immediately. As my wife and I moved into another room to give them some privacy, I heard the instructor ask my daughter, "So what song do you want to learn how to play?" She was in good hands.

The Fun equation, though not a formal business practice, is a part of human nature. I have seen smaller companies who recognize this and integrate it into their DNA. I have seen larger organizations where there are pockets of fun, usually generated by younger leaders who get this axiom. Create a culture where fun is fostered and appreciated. Remember, this is not fun for fun's sake but an environment with a purpose in mind. Learning and training needs to be budgeted for and supported. Teaching, presenting, and applying new skills to current projects assists employees with retaining knowledge. Retention becomes part of the team dynamic and success is the byproduct.

With all this talk of fun, I want you to return to your roots as we near the end. Being a new leader may mean you are no longer *executing creative work*, but it does not mean you are no longer *creative at work*. Let us not forget to make time for being creative.

Chapter 39
Setting Aside Creative Time

I had the recent opportunity to attend a Design Thinking workshop led by several professors, lecturers, and design leaders from the Stanford Design School or d.school. If you are familiar with design thinking, you likely know the process or methodology used:

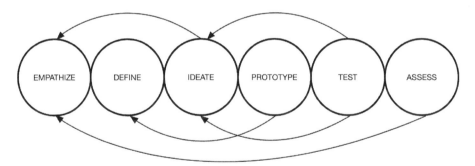

While this method looks linear, at all points during the process you are learning and discovering. This discovery process can lead you back a single step, several steps, or starting over again from the beginning. What comes intuitively for many designers, *Design Thinking* attempts to teach those from a non-design background. I will not go into detail here as there are volumes of information on the topic you can find for yourself. If you are not accustomed to Design Thinking, I would recommend spending some time learning about it and taking a workshop.

On this particular day, there was about forty of us going through the workshop. The tools which d.school staff presented have been refined over the years. The overarching goal of this workshop was to train the trainer. Other attendees and I were learning to train employees in our organization how to think like designers.

Interestingly, having taught on the subject myself, I was more intrigued by the new tools d.school had to offer. Then one of the professors said something profound—something I already knew but had fallen away from. He said, "Sometimes to be creative, you have to stop being creative. You have to walk away. That is why we have several mandatory breaks during our workshop. We want you to get out of the office, house, or workspace and go for a walk."

What? Who has time for a walk? I have so many hours I need to put in and while this workshop is nice, I still have projects and deadlines to get to. As I mentioned in an earlier chapter, I have an entrepreneurial bent. Having had my own company, I learned early on you have to *beat the street* to get work and then you have to *stay in your seat* to get it done. Who has time for a walk during a busy workday?

During this autotelic experience, I noticed several things. I got exercise, my mind focused on other issues while my subconscious processed the workshop, and I felt refreshed as blood and oxygen activated my brain, providing me with additional neural stimulation.

Upon my return, I had almost a dozen new ideas addressing the workshop problem. I was energized and able to contribute as much or more than the morning session—all by taking a short fifteen-minute walk!

How had I forgotten this simple idea?

Take Time Off

As a creative leader I had forgotten *to be* creative. Not *how to be* creative but to allow creativity to naturally extend from who I am and how I was uniquely made. I realized after being in leadership for so long, I had found myself more focused on productivity: deadlines, to-do lists, and meetings. I forgot to build in much needed down time. As I looked back over my year, I had taken very little time off. I still had between 150-175 hours of personal time. Why had I let that happen? Lack of focus and balance does not happen overnight. It happens slowly over time when we forget what is truly important and chase after urgent, less meaningful things.

This may be one of the biggest boosts to creativity you can ever have! But it requires discipline. Set time on your calendar daily or, if you feel that is too radical, set up something weekly. I have weekly "learning time" built into my schedule during Fridays—typically a slower day for me. Also, set aside personal time away from the office and home. Take a vacation, visit a museum, go to a bookstore, hike/bike a trail and bring along something to capture notes and ideas. It could be a small sketchbook or your smartphone. Get away and let your subconscious go to work.

The Unconscious Mind and Creativity

In their book, *Creative Confidence*, Tom and David Kelley say, "Our brains are constantly making connections and associations with people, things, and ideas we come in contact with. Don't let those serendipitous ideas go to waste." [80]

This is common among creatives. When creativity is forced, it sometimes produces quality work. More often, after information and design problems simmer, the creative unconscious mind goes to work. Dr. Nancy C. Andreasen describes this process in her paper, *A Journey Into Chaos: Creativity and The Unconscious*: [81]

> The creative process moves through stages. It begins with preparation, a time when the basic information or skills are assembled. It continues on to incubation, a relaxed time during which the person does not work consciously to solve the problem, but when connections are unconsciously being made. This then leads eventually to inspiration, the eureka experience when the person suddenly sees the solution. It ends with production, a time when the insights are put into a useful form.

When these unconscious ideas manifest is different for each person. Some have their "aha" moments when exercising, running, or swimming. Others while they are relaxing, playing games, driving or in the shower. David Kelley says he keeps a dry erase marker in the shower to write down ideas when they come to him.[82] These examples tell us about *where/when* epiphanies can strike but not *how* they are born.

Several studies turn to the concepts of self-organizing systems and Chaos Theory. Dr. Andreasen postulates:[83]

> Chaos theory, also known as complexity theory, is the study of dynamic and nonlinear processes and of self-organising systems (Gleick, 1987). Self-organising systems can be seen all around us, once we begin to look for them. We see them in the flocking of birds, the schooling of fish and the changing global ecosystem. All these things produce a form of organisation in which the control is not centralised, but rather is distributed throughout the entire system. The system is dynamic, and changes arise spontaneously and frequently produce something new. Seen within this context, the human brain is the ultimate self-organising system, and creativity is one of its most important emergent properties.

While this is one idea, it seems more likely that our cognitive processes have more to do with creative expression. Because of our sensitivities to our surroundings, creatives process large amounts of information just below the surface—in our unconscious mind. Dr. Albert Rothenberg, psychiatry professor at Harvard Medical School, more recently suggests:[84]

> Discovery of the cognitive homospatial, janusian, and sep-con articulation processes in creativity... help to show the reason for the sense of unawareness as well as the presence of some degree of unconscious manifestations. None of these processes appear directly in awareness, and none arise directly from unconscious sources. None, however, follow the patterns of ordinary stepwise or productive thinking. With all

three of these processes, creators are only consciously aware of the products of their thinking. Only the resulting metaphor, characterization, plot idea, visual image, musical phrase, or theoretical formulation appears in consciousness, not the structural features of these processes such as searching for opposites (janusian process), superimposing mental images (homospatial process) or separating with connecting (sep-con articulation process). Because the creators are not aware (and do not need to be aware) of the structure of their thinking and seldom if ever retrace particular thought sequences leading to creative ideas, the ideas seem to them to result from factors out of their control. All retain the qualities of nonconscious types of thought.

Many creatives cannot describe how their creative process works. Yes, there are tools and practices (which we will discuss shortly) that help facilitate the process, but the "eureka" instances are frequently the results of empathetic and adaptable thinking. Creatives demonstrate this unusual process more than others. Get excited, you are a rare and unique individual that sees the world differently, and so are the members of your team.

Neuroplasticity and Creativity

Contrary to previous beliefs, our brains can continue to learn, grow, and make new connections throughout our lifetime. Neuroplasticity or neural plasticity is our brain's ability to adapt and change, forming new neural connections over time. Whenever you store memories, learn new skills, are psychologically stressed, influenced by your environment, or consume information, your brain's network and circuits change. This is good news.

As recommended earlier, be a lifelong learner. New relationships, new activities, new places to go, new books to read, and new hobbies to learn all build your knowledge base from which your inventiveness draws. Pushing our mental focus and attention grows areas of the brain. Let's never forget to use and exercise our creative muscles, because if we do not use it, we *can* lose it.

Use It or Lose It

Just like the computer saying "garbage in, garbage out," our brain and thought life are similar. What we think about and how often we think about certain topics get the most space in our brains. Are you regularly exercising your creative muscles? Below are a few exercises I have found fun and helpful over the years. You can do these individually or as a team.

Exercises

Find these exercises and others in the *Creatives Lead Companion Workbook*.

Mind Mapping - This exercise allows you to get ideas out of your head quickly. You can use a whiteboard or piece of paper. In the center you will put your central idea and then branch out, jotting down associated ideas. Each of these associated ideas will spawn additional thoughts. This is something you can return to later and add to or investigate for connections between ideas that form larger themes. Give yourself fifteen minutes and see how many ideas you can generate.

Sketching - A go-to for many creatives is a sketchbook. Use one to sketch out ideas and concepts. You do not need to worry about the quality of the sketch, just draw a visual representation of the thoughts and ideas you are trying to capture. These too you can visit later for additional insights. I suggest getting a sketchbook that is small enough to carry with you. When ideas hit, you will be glad you have it to capture your next innovation.

Idea file/mood board - I have also used my sketchbook for collecting ideas, images, photos, patterns, typography, and colors. These tend to be more thematic in nature as you create a mood, vibe, or some kind of brand association. I'll even tape magazine cutouts and product labels onto pages—anything to spark or capture ideas. This exercise allows you to keep a creative record you can always return to for inspiration.

Combine ideas - This exercise allows you to review a series of thoughts and images while looking for ways to combine them into something new and unique. Take past ideas and mash them together. Make something new. What connections can you make between two opposite or miscellaneous ideas? Give yourself thirty to forty minutes to see how many fresh ideas you come up with.

Go to extremes - I got this idea years ago from Mark Oldach's book, *Creativity for Graphic Designers.* [85] Look at things from the other end. If you are used to looking at something from one side, turn it around or on its side or upside down. The same thing applies to concepts. Approach them from a fresh perspective. "If something demands to be white, try making it black. If something is normally stated in words, substitute numbers. Don't keep a piece of type small, make it enormous," Oldach suggests.

30 circles - This exercise was shared by Bob McKim, who mentored David Kelley. Taking a sheet of paper draw 30 circles. Next, make each of those circles into something recognizable like a ball or flower or smiley. How many can you complete in three minutes? Did you or anyone think of combining circles? Try this exercise with the team and then share your circles.

Play with words - This was one of my favorite exercises in art school. Take two words and think of some creative idea as the merger between them. For instance, take *tree* and *mollusk*—what thoughts and ideas comes to mind? A tree of snails? A snail that sprouts a tree? Sir Issac Newton sitting under the mollusk tree? Have fun and see where this leads.

Image exploration - As you sketch out ideas or images, what additional shapes come to mind? How might something look in a square shape or *as a box*? What about a circular shape, triangle, or rectangle? Confining, expanding, and squishing images gives rise to new thoughts and ideas. Try making something three-dimensional. Next, draw it from a different point of view: low, high, worms-eye view, eagles-eye view, close up or far away.

Squiggle exploration - This exercise I have done and taught others for years. I honestly do not know where this first originated. Use a piece of paper and draw a random "squiggle" on it. Next, use the squiggle as a starting point for an image or illustration. Can you use the same squiggle and come up with multiple ideas? Try it by yourself and with the team and see how many ideas you can generate. Example: Below are three squiggles I made. I used squiggle number three and created three variations from it below.

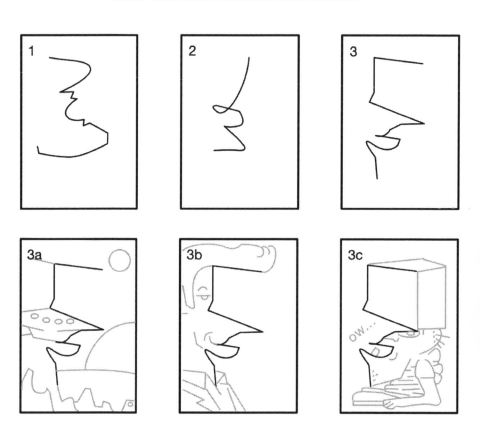

As a creative leader, you may no longer be an individual contributor, but you are still creative. Use your creativity to mentor team members, review work and ideas, and push and encourage employees to be their best. Remember to carve out regular time to grow, learn, and let your creative juices flow. You are uniquely you. There is no one else who looks at the work and problems the same as you do. Be proud of all the work you have done up to this point. Leading a team, and creating an amazing culture can be a joy or can be drudgery. A lot of it is up to you. My hope is that this book has provided you with key insights and resources for an exciting career of creative leadership. Now, let's turn the page and put this last week into application.

Applications for Week 12

Creativity is a secret to success. No matter what you approach in life, approach it from a creative perspective. Whether it be working remotely, injecting Fun into the workplace, or taking time off to recharge—use it as a creative exercise and keep building for the future.

Practical Applications

I want you to finish strong this week. Your long-term trajectory hinges on what you do from here on out. There are four applications, but the last one—the quarterly self-assessment—is most important. You have had a three-month run in your new role. It's time to assess, course correct, make possible personnel decisions, and set up a cadence for a quarterly review.

1. Look into your remote working policies.
2. Weave fun into your team culture.
3. Pick several creative exercises to try this week—alone or with the team.
4. Take the *Creatives Lead Quarterly Growth Indicator©*.

Remote Work Policy

Get with your Human Resources department and learn what remote work policies you have available for the team. Make sure your technology department can support employees with access to Virtual Private Networks (VPN) as well as the collaborative tools remote workers will need.

Weave Fun into Culture

During the next team meeting, empower the team to weave fun into their work. Brainstorm ideas or, better yet, let the team brainstorm on their own and come back to you with their thoughts and ideas. Next, put some or all the ideas into action.

Creativity Exercises

Set aside time this week to personally practice several of the exercises. Explore more on your own. The *Creatives Lead Companion Workbook* has additional exercises and sheets for you to copy and use. Try some during your team meetings as a way to keep the creative spark bright.

If you do an exercise with the team, time-box the session. Afterward, turn the remaining time into show-and-tell. Ask and encourage questions:

- What did you come up with?
- How many ideas did you generate?
- Describe your thinking process.

Quarterly Growth Indicator

You have been going through this book for the last three months. Let's see how you are doing. Below is the *Creatives Lead Quarterly Growth Indicator* reviewing the principles you have begun putting into practice. Review each statement and rate it low to high based on how well you have assimilated the practice into your life and leadership.

A score of 90-100 = You are amazing and the envy of your peers and other leaders.

A score of 75-89 = You are off to a great start! Work on focus and balance.

A score of 50-74 = You have growth areas. Make a plan to improve these areas over the next quarter.

A score of 25-49 = Do not be too hard on yourself. Work on one area at a time until it becomes a habit.

ASSESSMENT	Low-Scoring-High			
I know the temperaments of everyone on the team.	1	2	3	4
I know the career goals of each team member.	1	2	3	4
I know my strengths and weaknesses as a leader.	1	2	3	4
I know the strengths and weaknesses of each team member.	1	2	3	4

I genuinely care for each person on the team.	1	2	3	4
I know my communication style and the styles of the team members.	1	2	3	4
I communicate well and set expectations.	1	2	3	4
I do not micromanage.	1	2	3	4
I handle team issues quickly and carefully.	1	2	3	4
Exercise is important to me.	1	2	3	4
I work out every week.	1	2	3	4
I get proper rest each night.	1	2	3	4
I eat healthy.	1	2	3	4
I like to have fun at work.	1	2	3	4
I encourage the team to have fun at work.	1	2	3	4
I balance my time well.	1	2	3	4
I am productive.	1	2	3	4
The team is productive.	1	2	3	4
I have time to focus on my most important projects.	1	2	3	4
I collaborate well.	1	2	3	4
I am giving my leadership power away.	1	2	3	4
I am mentoring someone.	1	2	3	4
I am intentionally leaving a legacy.	1	2	3	4
The team culture is healthy and growing.	1	2	3	4
I set aside creative time regularly.	1	2	3	4
TOTAL SCORE				

Finally, I was given this series of questions from a friend. You will find that these questions cut across all aspects of life. I have written them on an index card and keep them on my desk. I hope you find them as beneficial as I have over the years.

Six Questions

1. What areas of my thinking do I need to change?
2. What beliefs do I hold that hold me back?
3. What expectations hinder my personal growth?
4. What attitudes hurt my success?
5. What behavioral areas must change to give me a boost?
6. What things are keeping me from peak performance?

Conclusion
An Uncommon Journey

The last twelve weeks have flown by. As you have been reading and applying this book, there are likely questions that have come up. Never fear. I think you will find that as you form healthy leadership habits, you will know what to do in different circumstances. After all, much of leading is really common sense.

- Leadership Lessons From Leonidas
- Take The Next Step

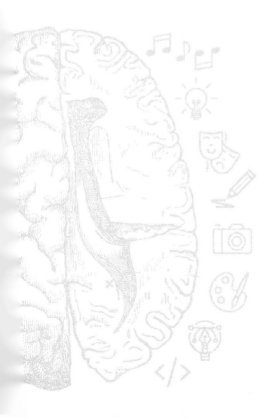

Chapter 40

Leadership Lessons From Leonidas

I recently read the book *Gates of Fire* by Steven Pressfield, upon which the graphic novel and movie *300* were based. Toward the latter part of the book the narrator describes what a true king is. The author's thoughts here were profound to say the least and can be directed at every modern-day leader who has the courage, valor, humility, grace, and heroic opportunity to lead.

I hope you are challenged and inspired by the comparisons below:

> I will tell His Majesty what a king is. A king does not abide within his tent while his men bleed and die upon the field. A king does not dine while his men go hungry, nor sleep when they stand at watch upon the wall. A king does not command his men's loyalty through fear nor purchase it with gold; he earns their love by the sweat of his own back and the pains he endures for their sake. That which comprises the harshest burden, a king lifts first and sets down last. A king does not require service of those he leads but provides it to them. He serves them, not they him.[86]

Likewise…

I will tell you of a superior leader. A leader does not go home early when her employees are still hard at work on key company projects. A leader does not eat out at the finest restaurants while her employees have only stipend enough for fast food, nor is she cavalier about directing the organization while employees see potential issues ahead. A leader does not demand loyalty by positional power or by threats and bribery; she earns their respect, admiration, and love by taking initiative, communicating, and shielding them from harsh business realities. The leader leads by example—she doesn't need to have the premier parking space and is not so proud that she won't get down on the front line herself—working long and hard. A leader is not in her position to be served but to serve her employees, board members, and stockholders. She is a leader worth following. She is a Creative Leader.

Chapter 41

Take the Next Step

"Common sense ain't common." - Will Rogers

"Seek advice but use your own common sense" - Yiddish Proverb

"Nothing is more fairly distributed than common sense: no one thinks he needs more of it than he already has." - Rene Descartes

"Common sense is the knack of seeing things as they are, and doing things as they ought to be done." - C.E. Stowe (Son of the late Harriet Beecher Stowe)

In this concluding chapter, we will review. A major part of forming habits is reflecting on what you want to remember. You will recall some of these ideas as being common sense, but application is where true creative leadership begins. Let's review the practices we have covered one last time.

"Measure Twice, Cut Once"

If you've ever done woodworking, this is a common phrase. The application is to double-check yourself before you commit to a final cut. If you have measured wrong, then you'll have to discard the wood and get another piece to start all over again. This same principle applies in hiring.

Too often we rush the process in order to fill a spot. When you rush a hire you run the risk of getting the wrong person for the job.

I encountered this very thing when hiring for a position that I had open for over six months. I hired someone who turned out to be the wrong fit and caused issues with the entire department. Had I heeded this common sense principle, I would have spared myself and the team a lot of grief. Take the time to measure the potential employee and double-check before you extend a final offer.

Past Behavior Is a Predictor

Promoting from the inside is not a bad practice depending on the business situation. Granted, sometimes you might need new blood to stir things up but, more often than not, promoting from within is a good common sense practice.

When looking at employees for promotion, evaluate their past behavior and performance. If an employee cuts corners, common sense says that moving this person into a manager role will not change this behavior. If anything, this behavior will cause more issues at a senior level than it did in the previous position. The poor behavior is intensified. If you feel an employee has leadership capabilities, give them short-term projects that put them in a leadership role. Watch how they handle people and the project. If an employee shows consistent integrity and responsibility over time and they have good relationships with staff, then this might be your person for promotion. Remember, past behavior can be a predictor for future behavior.

People Over Process

Your biggest asset in any organization is the people. Yet, you will not believe how many employees in companies are treated second-rate and taken for granted. Most managers focus on things rather than ideas, but it all starts with ideas. Ideas come from people. Focus on managing ideas if you want to take your team to the next level.

Creativity is directly tied to ideas, and all people are creative. If you mine for creativity, you experience innovation and that opens the door to all kinds of business improvements. The leader that understands this will hang onto employees. The leader that does not understand that their people come first will lose ideas and eventually people. Common sense says treat people the way you want to be treated and value them over things.

My Way or the Highway

No company is immune to conflict, and no one likes dealing with it. Those who say they have no problem dealing with conflict usually fire offending parties and move on. Not a good practice. You, as a creative leader, may be having a bad day and say or do something you regret. Do you want to be let go or be given another opportunity?

It is easy to put off dealing with issues that arise, but the fact is we need to hit them head-on. We should not dance around the subject but work on it and work through it. Make sure you have all the facts, and try to remain neutral as you listen attentively to all sides. A screaming tirade does nothing but distance yourself and put up barriers. Treat all parties with respect and try to handle conflict privately and in a mature, professional manner. Remember, people are your greatest resource.

Go Team Go

The simple truth is you can never accomplish with one person what you can accomplish with a team. A common sense principle is to form teams where members compensate for one another's weaknesses. Then let the team be part of the goal-setting process. Who is not motivated when they are included as part of the brainstorming and goal setting for an initiative?

Myron Rush said it well–each team member has four key needs that must be met by fellow team members. These needs are to use one's skills to assist the team effort, to be accepted as part of the team, to have personal goals compatible with team goals, and to represent people and groups outside the team. These needs must be met in order for a person to feel they are making a meaningful contribution.

Let's Talk About It

Another key principle is communication—clear, consistent, and constant communication. Communication is the lifeblood of every organization and team. Without it, relationships die. But, wait, weren't we talking about communication? What do relationships have to do with that? Relationships are foundational to and a byproduct of communication. Try not talking to your co-workers, your friends, your children, your spouse and see what happens. Or like we so often do at work, try talking to them every now and then with minimal feedback and depth of conversation. Get the picture? Not a pretty sight, huh?

Common sense says, "Sure, communication is hard and there are often barriers; but the speaker and the listener both have a role to play." The speaker must know what they want to say and to say it clearly, accurately, and simply. The listener needs to listen attentively to the words and the message behind the words. Both need to be slow to speak and keen to listen objectively. We all want to be heard, so take time to learn to listen first. Only then will relationships and organizations grow and mature.

Delegate, Delegate, Delegate

Every manager needs to learn to delegate more often. You cannot do it all and you cannot do it by yourself (see Go Team Go above). To be effective in delegating, pick the right person to take the responsibility—remember, past behavior is a predictor. If you do not learn to delegate, you are no more than a worker yourself and not a leader. Come on, this is common sense. You cannot maintain control over every little aspect. Entrust key projects to trusted people, set the expectations and boundaries, and then move on to do your job.

"How' You Doin'?"

Yes, Joey used this as a pick-up line in the sitcom, *Friends*, yet the question is relevant to us all in regard to work. We often have exasperating thoughts when it comes to performance evaluation. Why? Could it be the process is ineffectual? Often, managers evaluate on the past. What good does that do since you cannot change past failures? Do you like being evaluated this way yourself? It is a common sense principle to check and evaluate *as you go*. Evaluate the performance of the employee as they are working on or finishing up a project. This should be an open time of learning for you both. The employee can learn from you what they did well and what they need improvement on. You can learn from the employee what you did well and need improvement on. Don't be so arrogant, since you're the leader, to think that you know it all. With this kind of *ongoing* performance evaluation, everybody wins.

Cultural Impact

Creating and reinforcing team culture is paramount to your legacy as a leader. The team rises and falls on the culture you create. No matter the culture you came from or experienced in your past, you need to create a healthy and vibrant one for your team. A culture of ownership, fun, creativity, integrity, accountability, mutual trust, and responsibility is what you desire. You want to work in this kind of environment and so do your teammates. This kind of culture is common sense—attractive and propels you past any short-term failures. This kind of culture will have other employees wanting to work with you while other leaders envy you.

Creatives Lead

As you can see from all the practices above, common sense is often asking you to look at business, work, and life from another's perspective: owner, boss, employee, vendor, partner, or customer. It is not hard to *know* what to do, but it is often hard to *do it*. Think of creative leadership as a journey, and set off on the next part of the path today. You can do it—one step at a time. You know this to be true. You are off to a great start. You have new tools in your creative tool belt.

Now, shout it at the top of your lungs, "*CREATIVES LEAD*" and take *that* next step. You've got this!

Acknowledgements

Writing a book is hard work. It takes a lot of mental and emotional effort. There are times when you wonder, "Is this going to help anyone?" and then you let a few people read some early chapters and they respond with, "This is great—all new leaders need this material!" That feels like a booster shot and keeps you going for another month. After a while you get tired of reading your words and wonder if you should even be working on the project. Then you talk to a subject matter expert who says, "This speaks right to my situation!" and the cycle repeats. If you have written a book, you know exactly what I am talking about. It is a learning experience and a labor of love.

Here is my feeble attempt to thank all of the wonderful people who had a hand in encouraging me and making this book better for the sake of the reader. In no particular order, I want to acknowledge and thank:

My family and wife, Sharon, who put up with the long hours of writing and editing while "holding down the fort." She was also my first reader.

My editor, Brooke, for all the ideas, encouragement, and insights. Not to mention the terrific job she did editing. She was the first to believe in this project and I am grateful.

My brother-in-law, Matt Hale, for his unmatched proofreading skills. You are a creative in many ways.

Thank you, Nichole Fogel, for your amazing writing and editing of marketing material. You went above and beyond.

Thank you, R.J. Patterson, for taking my phone call and being willing to answer all my newbie author questions. I will likely be calling again.

Thank you to Jennifer Allison for her encouragement and insights on self-publishing. I am grateful for her friendship and creative spirit.

My Alpha Readers: Aida, Ben, Diane, Linda, Sharon, and Tiff. You were a huge help and dear friends to willingly submit yourselves to the initial read. Your feedback and comments were enlightening and helped take the manuscript to the next level.

Thank you to the business leaders and subject matter experts I sent early chapters to who approved the content and direction: Dr. Anthony Balduzzi, Caroline Samalin, Chad Williams, Dennis Worden, Dr. John Trent, Linda Demaris, and Todd Samalin.

Thank you to my launch team who helped promote the initial release of this book and were willing to be my advocates:

Jennifer Allison, Kelsy Black, Kim Brockman, Linda Demaris, Diane DeSeta, Brian Edwards, Loubna Fassi, Ben Fogel, Nichole Fogel, Keith Freck, James Gray, Joe Guthrie, Lisa Hale, Matt Hale, John Hollis, Joy Howell, Patrick Hoydar, Jiawei Hu, Amy Hultquist, Dan Hultquist, Jennifer Kendrick, Joy Llena, Paul Martin, Rebecca Martin, Felipe Niada, Seth Rexilius, Pashonia Robinson, Marc Roth, Tammy Roth, Caroline Samalin, Tiff Schank, Ben Schoer, Carla Scruggs, Kiel Shaw, Michael Shelley, Linda Sorrow, Ashley Spencer, Gina Taylor, Jerry Tracey, Brooke Turbyfill, Joani Veenstra, Shelli Wheeler, Katy Wise, Dennis Worden. You are all heroes.

Recommended Reading

Anderson, Gretchen. *Mastering Collaboration: Make Working Together Less Painful and More Productive.* Sebastopol: O'Reilly Media Inc., 2019.

Baber, Anne and Lynne Waymon. *Make Your Contacts Count: Networking Now-How for Cash, Clients, and Career Success (2nd Edition).* New York: AMACOM, 2007.

Blanchard, Ken and Michael O'Connor. *Managing By Values.* San Francisco: Berrett-Koehler Publishers, Inc., 1997.

Buford, Bob. *Half Time: Changing Your Game Pam From Success to Significance.* Grand Rapids, Zondervan Publishing House, 1994.

Buckingham, Marcus. *First Break All The Rules.* New York: Gallup Press, 2016.

Buckingham, Marcus. *Now Discover Your Strengths.* New York: Free Press, 2001.

Catmull, Ed. *Creativity, Inc.: Overcoming the Unseen Forces That Stand in the Way of True Inspiration.* New York: Random House, 2014.

Cialdini, Robert B. PhD. *Influence: The Psychology of Persuasion.* New York: Harper Business, 2006.

Clear, James. *Atomic Habits.* New York: Avery, 2018.

Collins, Jim. *Good to Great.* New York: Harper Business, 2001.

Covey, Stephen M. R. *The Speed of Trust: The One Thing That Changes Everything.* New York: Franklin Covey, 2008.

Depree, Max. *Leadership is an Art.* New York: Currency, 2004.

Dweck, Carol S. *Mindset: The New Psychology of Success.* New York: Random House, 2016.

Edelman, Kathleen. *I Said This You Heard That.* Atlanta: North Point Ministries Inc., 2019.

Ferriss, Timothy. *The 4-Hour Work Week.* New York: Harmony, 2009.

Finzel, Hanz. *Top 10 Mistakes Leaders Make.* Colorado Springs: Cook, 2000.

Gladwell, Malcolm. *Talking to Strangers.* New York: Little Brown and Co., 2019.

Goldratt, Eliyahu and Jeff Fox. *The Goal: A Process of Ongoing Improvement.* Barrington: North River Press, 2004.

Harnish, Verne. *Mastering The Rockefeller Habits.* New York: Select Books Inc., 2002.

Harvard Business Essentials. *Coaching and Mentoring.* Boston: Harvard Business Press, 2004.

Hesselbein, Frances. *Leader to Leader: Enduring Insights on Leadership From The Drucker Foundation's Award Winning Journal.* San Francisco: Jossey-Bass, 1999.

Kelley, Tom and Said Kelley. *Creative Confidence.* New York: Crown Business, 2013.

Kjerulf, Alexander. *Happy Hour is 9 to 5: How to Love Your Job, Love Your Life, and Kick Butt at Work.* Frederiksberg: Woohoo Press, 2006.

Kotter, John P. *Leading Change.* Boston: Harvard Business School Press, 1996.

Kouzes, James and Barry Posner. *The Leadership Challenge.* San Francisco: Jossey-Bass, 1995.

Lencioni, Patrick. *The Advantage: Why Organizational Health Trumps Everything Else in Business.* San Francisco: Jossey-Bass, 2012.

Lencioni, Patrick. *The Five Dysfunctions of a Team.* San Francisco: Jossey-Bass, 2002.

Lencioni, Patrick. *The Four Obsessions of an Extraordinary Executive.* San Francisco: Jossey-Bass, 2003.

Lencioni, Patrick. *Death By Meeting.* San Francisco: Jossey-Bass, 2004.

Lencioni, Patrick. *Silos, Politics, and Turf Wars.* San Francisco: Jossey-Bass, 2006.

Lynn, Adele B. *The EQ Difference.* New York: AMACOM, 2005.

Makenzie, Alec and Pat Nickerson. *The Time Trap* (3rd Ed.) New York: AMACOM, 2009.

Miller, Dan. *48 Days to the Work You Love.* Nashville: B&H Publishing, 2007.

Navarro, Joe and Marvin Karlins. *What Every Body Is Saying: An Ex-FBI Agent's Guide to Speed-Reading People.* New York: William Marrow Paperbacks, 2008.

Oldach, Mark. *Creativity for Graphic Designers.* Cincinnati: North Light Books, 1995.

Peterson, Jordan. *12 Rules for Life: An Antidote to Chaos.* Toronto: Random House Canada, 2018.

Pink, Daniel H. *A Whole New Mind: Why Right-Brainers Will Rule the Future.* New York: Penguin Group, 2006.

Ramsey, Dave. *EntreLeadership: 20 Years of Practical Business Wisdom from The Trenches.* New York: Simon & Schuster, 2011.

Ries, Al. *Focus: The Future of Your Company Depends on It.* New York: HarperCollins, 1996.

Ries, Al and Jack Trout. *Horse Sense: How to Pull Ahead on the Business Track.* New York: Plume, 1992.

Rush, Myron. *Management: A Biblical Perspective.* Wheaton: SP Publications, 1983.

Silbiger, Steven. *The Ten Day MBA: A Step by Step Guide to Mastering the Skills Taught in America's Top Business Schools (Revised Edition).* NewYork: HarperCollins, 1999.

Smart, Bradford D. PhD. *Top Grading: The Proven Hiring and Promoting Method That Turbocharges Company Performance (3rd Edition).* New York: Portfolio, 2012.

Sonenshein, Scott. *Stretch: Unlock the Power of Less - and Achieve More Than You Ever Imagined.* New York: Harper Press, 2017.

Stack, Jack. *The Great Game of Business: Unlocking The Power and Profitability of Open-Book Management,* New York: DoubleDay, 1992.

Strasler, Steven. *MBA in a Day: What You Would Learn at the Top-Tier Business Schools.* Phoenix: Center for Professional Developement, 2004.

Swenson, Richard A. *Margin: Restoring Emotional, Physical, Financial, and Time Reserves to Overloaded Lives.* Colorado Springs: NavPress, 1992.

Watkins, Michael. *The First 90 Days: Critical Success Strategies for the New Leader.* Boston: Harvard Business Press, 1994.

Yates, Martin. *Hiring The Best: A Manager's Guide to Effective Interviewing.* Holbrook: Adams Media Corporation, 1994.

Notes

[1] Bruce W. Tuckman, *Developmental Sequence in Small Groups* (Psychological Bulletin, 1965), 63 (6): 384–399.

[2] Kathleen Edelman, *I Said This, You Heard That*: *How Your Wiring Colors Your Communication*, Workbook (Atlanta: North Point Ministries, Inc., 2018), 15.

[3] Martin Yates, *Hiring The Best: A Managers Guide to Effective Interviewing* (Holbrook: Adams Media Corporation,1994, 4th Edition), 55.

[4] Yates, *Hiring The Best*, 49.

[5] The STAR method often covers the following: Situation, Task, Action, and Result.

[6] Eliyahu Goldratt and Jeff Fox, *The Goal: A Process of Ongoing Improvement* (Great Barrington: The North River Press Publishing Corporation, 2004, Third Edition), chapter 15.

[7] "Overview of Learning Styles," *advanogy.com*, 2004, accessed February 7, 2021, https://www.learning-styles-online.com/overview/.

[8] Jeffrey J. Fox, *How to Become a Great Boss: The Rules for Getting and Keeping the Best Employees* (New York: Hyperion, 2002), 119.

[9] Dan Miller, *48 Days to The Work You Love* (Nashville: B&H Publishing, 2007), 88.

[10] Anne Baber and Lynne Waymon, *Make Your Contacts Count: Networking Know-How for Cash, Clients, and Career Success* (New York: AMACOM, 2002), 52-54.

[11] Patrick Lencioni, *The Four Obsessions of an Extraordinary Executive* (San Francisco: Jossey-Bass, 2000),150.

[12] Harry E. Chambers, *My Way or the Highway: The Micromanagement Survival Guide* (San Francisco: Berrett-Koehler Publishers, 2004), 141-170.

[13] Tim Dimoff, "9 Toxic Workplace Behaviors (and What to Do About Them)", *Mind Your Business,* (January 2019): 1 (online only), accessed November 15, 2020, https://www.cose.org/Mind-Your-Business/HR/9-Toxic-Workplace-Behaviors-and-What-to-Do-About-Them.

[14] Dimoff, *Mind Your Business:* 1 (online only).

[15] Dimoff, *Mind Your Business:* 1 (online only).

[16] Fox, *Great Boss*, 92.

[17] Arlene Semeco, MS, RD, "The Top 10 Benefits of Regular Exercise", *Healthline,* (February 2017): 1 (online only), accessed October 19, 2020, https://www.healthline.com/nutrition/10-benefits-of-exercise#TOC_TITLE_HDR_10.

"Exercise: 7 benefits of regular physical activity," Healthy Lifestyle, Mayo Foundation for Medical Education and Research, May 2019, https://www.mayoclinic.org/healthy-lifestyle/fitness/in-depth/exercise/art-20048389.

"Benefits of exercise," Live Well, NHS, June 2018, https://www.nhs.uk/live-well/exercise/exercise-health-benefits/.

[18] Northport Wellness Center, "The Importance of Good Nutrition," *Northport Wellness Center* (blog), *Your Path To Optimal Health*, August 11, 2016, https://www.northportwellnesscenter.com/blog/the-importance-of-good-nutrition.

[19] "Mental Health Resources for Adults," Health Direct, last reviewed April 2020, https://www.healthdirect.gov.au/adult-mental-health.

[20] Harvard Mental Health Newsletter, "Sleep and Mental Health: Sleep Deprivation Can Affect Your Mental Health," *Harvard Health Publishing,* updated March 18, 2019, health.harvard.edu/newsletter_article/sleep-and-mental-health.

[21] HealthLink British Columbia, "Mental and Emotional Benefits of Activity," *HealthLinkBC, British Columbia*, last reviewed November 2016, healthlinkbc.ca/physical-activity/mental-and-emotional-benefits.

[22] David H. Olson and Amy Olson, "Prepare/Enrich Program," Enrich Canada, Version 2000 (2000), accessed October 19, 2020, https://enrichcanada.ca/wp-content/uploads/2015/04/overview_v2000.pdf.

[23] "35 Years of Validation", About Prepare/Enrich, Prepare/Enrich, accessed February 14, 2021, https://www.prepare-enrich.com/webapp/pecv/about/template/DisplaySecureContent.vm;pc=1600554828919;jsessionid=8F417BC4FF10058285A0FC0624FD160E?id=pecv*about*research.html&xlat=Y&emb_org_id=0&emb_sch_id=0&emb_lng_code=ENGLISH.

[24] Natalie Butler, R.D., L.D., "What are some slow-release carbs?", *Medical News Today*, (June 2019): 1 (online only), accessed October 19, 2020, https://www.medicalnewstoday.com/articles/325586#fresh-fruits.

[25] Carolyn A. Hodges, R.D., "How to Meal-Prep a Week of High-Protein Lunches in 30 Minutes", *Eating Well,* (updated December 2019): 1 (online only), accessed October 19, 2020, https://www.eatingwell.com/article/291244/how-to-meal-prep-a-week-of-high-protein-lunches-in-30-minutes/.

[26] Alexander Kjerulf, *Happy Hour is 9 to 5: How to Love your Job, Love Your Life, and Kick Butt at Work* (Frederiksberg: Woohoo Press, 2006), 13.

[27] Kjerulf, *Happy Hour,* 163-184.

[28] Oscar Raymundo, "5 Reasons Googlers Think It's the Best Place to Work: In their own words, Google employee reveal what they love about life inside the 'Plex", *Inc. Work-Life Balance*, (December 2014): 1 (online only), accessed October 21, 2020, https://www.inc.com/oscar-raymundo/google-employees-best-place-to-work.html.

[29] Wikipedia, s.v. "Philippe Petit," last edited March 24, 2021, 14:10, https://en.wikipedia.org/wiki/Philippe_Petit.

Evan Bindelglass, "The Real Story Behind Philippe Petit's World Trade Center Hire-wire Stunt," *Curbed New York,* (September 2019), accessed

November 9, 2020, https://ny.curbed.com/2015/9/30/9916096/world-trade-center-philippe-petit-the-walk.

Jennifer Latson, "The High-Level Scheming Behind Philippe Petit's Twin Towers Tightrope Walk," *TIME,* (August 2015), accessed November 9, 2020, https://time.com/3976999/philippe-petit-twin-towers/.

30 Richard A. Swenson, M.D., *Margin: Restoring Emotional, Physical, Financial, and Time Reserves To Overloaded Lives* (Colorado Springs: NavPress, 1992), 216.

31 Swenson, *Margin,* 217.

32 Dr. Swenson credits this concept to an article by Richard H. Bube entitled "On the Pursuit of Excellence: Pitfalls in the Effort to Become No. 1." (1987), 70-71.

33 George Rust, M.D., *The Balancing Act* (Christian Medical Society Journal, 1983), 8.

34 Myron Rush, *Management: A Biblical Approach* (Wheaton: SP Publications, 1983), 221-227.

35 Rush, *Management,* 226.

36 Rush, *Management,* 227-230.

37 Rush, *Management,* 232.

38 Al Ries, *Focus: The Future of Your Company Depends on It* (New York: HarperCollins, 1996, First paperback edition), 74-82.

39 Ries, *Focus,* 76.

40 Ries, *Focus,* 79.

41 Beverage Digest, *Special Issue: Top-10 CSD Results for 2008* Archived April 19, 2009. Wayback Machine. Accessed November 16, 2020. https://web.archive.org/web/20090419085508/http://www.beverage-digest.com/pdf/top-10_2009.pdf.

42 Wikipedia, s.v. "Gil Amelio," last edited March 2, 2021, 08:38, https://en.wikipedia.org/wiki/Gil_Amelio.

43 Wikipedia, s.v. "Copland (operating system)," last edited March 7, 2021, 22:30, https://en.wikipedia.org/wiki/Copland_(operating_system).

44 Wikipedia, s.v. "Mac OS 8," last edited March 2, 2021, 12:22, https://en.wikipedia.org/wiki/Mac_OS_8.

45 Walter Isaacson, *Steve Jobs* (New York: Simon & Schuster, 2011), 336.

46 Isaacson, *Steve Jobs*, 339.

47 Ries, *Focus,* xiii.

48 Francesco Cirillo, *Do More and Have Fun With Time Management.* Accessed November 16, 2020. https://francescocirillo.com/pages/pomodoro-technique.

49 "Clint's Story", About Clint Pulver, *ClintPulver.com*, accessed November 16, 2020, https://clintpulver.com/about/.

50 Gretchen Anderson, *Mastering Collaboration: Making Working Together Less Painful and More Productive* (Sebastopol: O'Reilly Media Inc., 2019), Introduction 15.

51 Anne Truitt Zelenka, "Knowledge Economy (Drucker) vs Web Economy," *annezelenka.com* (private blog), June 2007, https://annezelenka.com/2007/06/knowledge-economy-drucker-vs-web-economy-zelenka.

52 Anderson, *Mastering Collaboration,* Introduction 15.

53 Michael Watkins, *The First 90 Days: Critical Success Strategies for New Leaders at All Levels* (Boston: Harvard Business School Publishing, 1994), 14.

54 Miller, *48 Days*, 19-20.

55 Wikipedia, s.v. "The Lone Ranger," last edited September 27, 2019, 17:03, https://en.wikiquote.org/wiki/The_Lone_Ranger.

56 Patrick Lencioni, *Overcoming The Five Dysfunctions of a Team: A Field Guide for Leaders, Managers, and Facilitators* (San Francisco: Jossey-Bass, 2005), 3.

[57] Carol S. Dweck, *Mindset: The New Psychology of Success* (New York: Random House, 2016), adapted from the diagram by Nigel Holmes.

[58] Adapted from Steven Strasler PhD, *MBA In A Day: What You Would Learn At Top-Tier Business Schools (If You Only Had The Time)* (Phoenix: Center for Professional Development Inc., 2004), 97-107.

[59] Ram Srinivasan, Terry Quan, and Pat Reed, *Accounting For Agile Projects*. Project Management Institute. Accessed November 16, 2020. https://www.pmi.org/learning/library/accounting-agile-projects-9303

[60] Steven Silbiger, *The Ten Day MBA Revised Ed.: A Step by Step Guide to Mastering The Skills Taught in America's Top Business Schools* (New York: HarperCollins Publishing, 1999), 79.

[61] Silbiger, *The Ten Day MBA*, 87-89.

[62] Dave Ramsey, *EntreLeadership: 20 Years of Practical Business Wisdom From The Trenches* (New York: Simon & Schuster, Inc., 2011), 9-10.

[63] Verne Harnish, *Mastering the Rockefeller Habits: What You Must Do to Increase The Value of Your Fast-Growth Firm* (New York: SelectBooks, Inc., 2002), 22-23.

[64] Harnish, *Mastering the Rockefeller Habits*, 30-31.

[65] Watkins, *The First 90 Days: Critical Success Strategies for New Leaders at All Levels*, 61-73.

[66] Bob Buford, *Half Time: Changing Your Game Plan from Success to Significance* (Grand Rapids: Zondervan Publishing House 1994), 17. Idea adapted from his epitaph statement

[67] Tim Elmore, "What Does it Mean to be a Life-Giving Leader," *Healthy Leaders*, (August 2019): 1 (online only), accessed March 29, 2021, https://healthyleaders.com/what-does-it-mean-to-be-a-life-giving-leader/.

[68] Jack Stack, *The Great Game of Business: Unlocking The Power and Profitability of Open-Book Management* (New York: DoubleDay, 1992), 204.

[69] Ramsey, *EntreLeadership,* 299.

[70] Fox, *Great Boss,* 87.

[71] Frances Hesselbein and Paul Cohen, *Leader to Leader: Enduring Insights on Leadership From The Drucker Foundation's Award Winning Journal* (San Francisco: Jossey-Bass, 1999), 217-218.

[72] Amy Unger, *Frances Hesselbein: A Lifetime of Leadership.* Lehigh Valley Style. Accessed December 5, 2020. https://lehighvalleystyle.com/people/features/frances-hesselbein-a-lifetime-of-leadership/

[73] Ramsey, *EntreLeadership,* 236.

[74] Ramsey, *EntreLeadership,* 227.

[75] Roy Maurer, *Study Finds Productivity Not Deterred by Shift to Remote Work.* Society of Human Resource Management. Accessed January 1, 2021. https://www.shrm.org/hr-today/news/hr-news/pages/study-productivity-shift-remote-work-covid-coronavirus.aspx

[76] Game-Based Learning: An x-Learn Perspective Paper, 2005, An x-Learn Perspective Paper supported by a grant from the e-Learning CONSORTIUM, Kurt Squire, PhD., University of Wisconsin-Madison, page 4.

[77] Ethan Mollick and Nancy Rothbard, "Mandatory Fun: Consent, Gamification and the Impact of Games at Work," abstract (Management Department, The Wharton School, University of Pennsylvania, 2014), 39, https://papers.ssrn.com/sol3/papers.cfm?abstract_id=2277103.

[78] Wikipedia, s.v. "Fun," last edited March 16, 2021, 21:15, https://en.wikipedia.org/wiki/Fun.

[79] *Merriam-Webster,* s.v. "knowledge (n.)," accessed March 28, 2021, https://www.merriam-webster.com/dictionary/knowledge.

[80] Tom Kelley and David Kelley, *Creative Confidence: Unleashing The Creative Potential Within Us All* (New York: Crown Business, 2013), 218.

[81] Nancy C. Andreasen, M.D., Ph.D., *A Journey Into Chaos: Creativity and The Unconscious.* National Center for Biotechnology Information. Accessed January 1, 2021. https://www.ncbi.nlm.nih.gov/pmc/articles/PMC3115302/

[82] Kelley and Kelley, *Creative Confidence*, 218.

[83] Andreasen, *Journey Into Chaos,* https://www.ncbi.nlm.nih.gov/pmc/articles/PMC3115302/

[84] Albert Rothenberg, M.D., "The Mystic of the Unconscious in Creativity," Unconscious, *Psychology Today* (blog), September 14, 2019, https://www.psychologytoday.com/us/blog/creative-explorations/201909/the-mystique-the-unconscious-in-creativity.

[85] Mark Oldach, *Creativity for Graphic Designers* (Cincinnati: North Light Books, 1995), 55.

[86] Steven Pressfield, *Gates of Fire: An Epic Novel of the Battle of Thermopylae* (New York: Bantam, 2005), 412.

About The Author

Eric H. Brown is passionate about next generation leaders. Having been in leadership for almost three decades, he is ardent about helping creatives transition from individual contributors to leaders. Because creativity is a major differentiator in today's corporate landscape he believes that more creatives should sit in leadership positions.

Photo by: Mr. Jeno Uche

Throughout his leadership career, Eric has honed the craft of building high-performing, multi-disciplinary creative departments. He's worked across mediums and industries. He's held nearly every role available in the creative department: art director, digital director, e-learning designer, experience architect, and digital strategist. He remembers—fondly, now—the fears he had as a new leader; among his many lessons learned, he's found 'adapt and change' to be most critical.

As the owner of a design boutique, Eric consulted for brands across the U.S., including Rockwell Collins, Hilton Hotels, Chick-fil-A, CDC Software, Sea Ray Boats, GeoLearning, and Lucent Technologies. He's been honored to be both a featured conference speaker and moderator. He's also the author of the Creatives Lead Companion Workbook and Creatives Lead Discussion Guide for Leaders, Mentors, and Facilitators. You'll find more of Eric's written work on leadership and creativity on his blog.

Work and life have taken Eric from coast to coast of the U.S., landing him in the Southeast, where he lives with his family today. He loves the balance he finds here; he and his family enjoy the fast pace of city life, the beauty of the mountains, and the serenity of the beach. Eric's passion to learn extends beyond his vocation. He received his black belt in Isshinryu Karate and was a private instructor for several years. Being a learner at heart, he has varied interests in music, cuisine, reading, writing, percussion, and painting.

Visit creativeslead.com to learn about more helpful resources, and be sure to leave Eric a note. He would love to hear from you.

Urgent Request

Thank You for Reading My Book!

If you have found this book to be helpful, would you do me a couple favors? They are simple, and will take very little effort on your part.

First, please leave me a helpful review on Amazon, GoodReads, LinkedIn, and any other social media. This will help make subsequent versions of this book and future books better.

Second, if anyone came to mind while you were reading this book, that you feel should know about it, and could benefit from it, would you tell them?

That's it.

Thanks for being awesome!
-Eric

1) Emotional calm, restraint ; not showing frustration

Saying calm under stress

2) 1 x 1 - giving feedback

· Helping people get unstuck

· Knowing the next step you need someone to take

- Knowing the right course of action / thing to do next

· Knowing what the end result should look like to be good / enough

- Giving creative feedback / direction

· Managing difficult clients

+ Visual formatting of presentations

Software - PS
          AI
          Sketch
          Figma

Imprv

Classes :
· Management skills
· Visual design
· Software
· Improv
+ Meditate / calm / pray

Made in the USA
Columbia, SC
28 August 2021